MW01258905

PRAI
THE POWER OF DIFFERENTIATION

"Brand differentiation isn't about being different for the sake of it; it's about being unforgettable, unignorable. This is a compelling read, peppered with insightful real-life examples and very relevant to any enterprise leader grappling with the disruptive challenges confronting businesses today."

> – Johan de Nysschen, President and CEO of ARRI Americas,
> Automotive industry visionary, Former CEO of Infiniti,
> President of Cadillac, President of Audi and
> COO of Volkswagen Group of America

"If you're looking to transform your brand and inspire your organization, look no further than *The Power of Differentiation*."

> – Anoop Prakash, EVP Americas, AriensCo

"The importance given to immersive, interactive, and dynamic learning is what differentiates Barry and what his teams can deliver. The ability to bring a brand to life through sensorial and tangible storytelling is what inspires people and drives advocacy."

> – Charlie Whitfield, Global Consumer & Internal
> Advocacy Lead, The Macallan

"No company can succeed without identifying and celebrating its unique competitive advantages. Barry provides a flight plan for your brand that will guide you to new heights."

> – Kenn Ricci, American aviation entrepreneur,
> Chairperson of Flexjet

CHRIS — BARRY IS A
GOOD FRIEND OF MINE, WHO,
I THINK, WILL BECOME A
KNOWN AND RESPECTED
BUSINESS INFLUENCER

THE **POWER** OF **DIFFERENTIATION**

ACROSS THE USA.

EN JOY !!

DAD

THE **POWER** OF
DIFFERENTIATION

Win Hearts, Minds, and Market Share

BARRY LABOV

The Power of Differentiation

Library of Congress Control Number: 2024905970

ISBN: 978-1-954676-86-2 (paperback)   978-1-954676-88-6 (ebook)
        978-1-954676-87-9 (hardcover)

Although this publication is designed to provide accurate information about the subject matter, the publisher and the author assume no responsibility for any errors, inaccuracies, omissions, or inconsistencies herein. This publication is intended as a resource, however, it is not intended as a replacement for direct and personalized professional services.

Images in this publication were provided by LABOV Marketing Communications and Training. www.labov.com

Editors: Tamzen Meyer, Jorge David Remy, and Nöella Simmons
Cover Design: Marcus McMillen, Matt Hakey, and Emma Elzinga
Interior Design: Emma Elzinga

Printed in the United States of America

First Edition
3 West Garden Street, Ste. 718
Pensacola, FL 32502
www.indigoriverpublishing.com

Ordering Information:

Quantity sales: Special discounts are available on quantity purchases by corporations, associations, and others. For details, contact the publisher at the address above.

Orders by US trade bookstores and wholesalers: Please contact the publisher at the address above.

With Indigo River Publishing, you can always expect great books, strong voices, and meaningful messages. Most importantly, you'll always find . . . *words worth reading.*

CONTENTS

INTRODUCTION

MY DAYS IN A 1980s ROCK BAND taught me much about leadership and what it takes to stand out from the crowd. The music industry has one of the fiercest competitive landscapes around, and "making it" demands differentiation—of your band and your sound. I experienced that challenge firsthand in the heyday of my band, Mark Urgent. While we didn't become a household name, we achieved some notoriety, with one of our songs featured on *American Bandstand* and reaching the *Billboard* charts. We couldn't have made it that far without having extraordinarily talented musicians and finding our own unique "sound" to differentiate us.

Fast forward to today. As the CEO of the marketing and training agency I founded in 1981, I've collaborated with business leaders for over four decades. I helped many to discover their own unique "sound" and excel at differentiating their products. I've also witnessed others with their spirits crushed as they desperately devalued the uniqueness of their products by lowering prices to gain market share. As this unfolded, their employees lost passion and pride, resulting in lower product quality and poor employee retention.

But it doesn't have to be like that. With over 500,000 brands in the world, the good news is yours doesn't have to claim to be the fastest, cheapest, or the best to succeed. You do need to discover what makes you who you are and celebrate it. In this book, I'll show you how manufacturing and service companies in diverse industries have done just that.

There's never been a more opportune or critical time to stand out from the pack. Today, because of the global reach of technology, such as the web, AI and social media, your products and services are pitted against competitors from all over the world. Those competitors likely make claims as to their superiority or better value.

Your personnel, likewise, are now more in demand and independent than ever. They seek meaning in what they do. During the pandemic, nearly fifty million Americans quit their jobs. Today, employees can work from home for companies located around the world or walk down the street to your competitor if they don't believe in your brand. When your brand, products, and services aren't differentiated, you will lose both customers *and* employees.

Throughout this book, I share stories of leaders who faced challenges along the journey to separate themselves from the competition. You'll feel the pride and passion they exhibited as they rallied their teams to, in many cases, make history with their brands.

Each chapter focuses on a specific aspect of differentiation and relates real-world accounts of a leader or company that encountered a challenge and how they overcame it. I also share a few personal stories, including my time as a youth sports coach, which illustrate the power of differentiation in all facets of our lives. The chapters are short and stand on their own, lending them to being easily shared with employees.

Because the success of every company is based on its people and their belief in the brand's differentiation, you will be introduced to my team and learn their role in helping our clients create uniqueness and meaning throughout their organizations. By the conclusion of this book, you will know and appreciate the wonderful, talented people with whom I've been blessed to work and play.

I dedicate this book to leaders who believe people are the answer, not the problem. These are the kinds of leaders who are brave enough to be vulnerable, to listen, and to inspire their enterprise to be uniquely its best. Let this fuel your own journey to differentiate. *Leaders differentiate.*

CHAPTER 1

WOULD YOU BUY YOUR OWN PRODUCT OR SERVICE?

"WE'RE FACING HEADWINDS that could shut us down." Ben, a beloved customer, continued. "I hate to dial your number because it's like reaching out to my attorney; it means I have an issue. Can you join me for a chat with my leadership team?" He was the CEO of a century-old manufacturing company that had been acquired numerous times. Slowly, but surely over the decades, their brand had become tarnished and devalued, not only in the industry, but in the eyes of its employees. It was currently considered a "me-too" product with no distinctiveness against its competitive set. Ben had been chosen by the company's board to lead them to the promised land.

We convened via phone a week later for an open discussion of their challenges. Rob, their VP of sales, voiced his opinion. "We know what's important to the industry: low price and on-time delivery. We're struggling with both."

The VP of engineering joined in. "We do nothing unique, nothing anyone else doesn't do." Their new manufacturing leader sadly added, "Our quality is poor, morale is low, we have a lot of problems."

After thirty minutes of enduring this not-so-uplifting conversation, I chimed in. "Based on what I've heard so far, not one of you would buy your own product."

After moments of dead silence, Ben spoke up. "You know, that's a really intriguing observation."

The sentiments shared by these executives are typical. It's a familiar theme from leaders who have been beaten down after futile attempts to turn the tide in their favor. There is great pressure to assume you're no different or better than anyone else, perhaps even inferior. In turn, that influences your employees to dismiss the value of the brand or product as well. This cycle wears you down, eventually eroding market share, product quality, service, and morale.

In the case of this century-old manufacturer, isn't it logical to think that they must have been doing or offering something of unique value to have survived this long? Yet their poor self-image reflected in the way their leaders spoke and behaved. But there was hope. Almost every brand can recover from this when they begin the journey to discover what makes them unique.

Under Ben's leadership, they embarked on a year-long crusade to reignite the brand and product line, while also instilling a culture of pride at its new, ultra-modern plant. Then came a make-or-break moment. They received an opportunity to bid on what would be the largest contract in their history. How they responded would be pivotal to success . . . or failure. As the bid negotiations progressed, I engaged numerous times with the team, hoping to spur them on to victory.

Those discussions began with them preparing to fail as they explained to me they really had few advantages against the competition. In fact, as they detailed the many reasons they could not win, I believed they were trying to "sell me" on them losing. Rob knew that if his sales team didn't believe, then the customer certainly would receive that message loud and clear as well. This had to end immediately.

Rob and I rolled up our sleeves and started to look for differentiation. We struck gold as we held an open conversation with the team, looking for any signs of hope. Their VP of service spoke up and shared that they had been providing *free* service to this customer for years. Their VP of engineering added that his team had designed product specifications (again for free) that the customer had then handed off to a competitor to produce. So, for the last few years, Ben and team had been supplying free service and engineering to this customer. That needed to count for something! And the longer we talked, the more evident it became that their product was best suited for the customer's mission. The team promised me they'd address these and other advantages in an upcoming meeting with the customer's decision-makers. I felt invigorated and confident that a breakthrough was about to happen.

I was wrong.

Rob called after the meeting and told me it had gone "south," as the customer constantly dismissed the various "extras" and value his company had been providing. To me, as an outsider listening to all this, it was clear that either the customer didn't value their differentiation at all or was just trying to negotiate. The team was deflated, but this is where a leader must step up and show conviction.

Rob decided he had nothing to lose; he would stand tall, call the customer back, and get real, asking her where the disconnect was between the two companies. After all, his team had been selflessly supporting them for years and had grown to know their needs better than anyone else. The customer confessed that she had issues with one of his sales reps who had allegedly made critical comments about how they had been servicing her company for free. Rob, showing his integrity, didn't throw his sales rep under the bus, but acknowledged it had been frustrating and moving forward, assuming they got the business, that would not be the case. Before hanging up, the customer admitted that Rob's bid was impressive and being taken seriously.

It wasn't long before I received a call as Rob excitedly shared. "Hey, I wanted to tell you we won the $40 million bid!" He then let me in on exactly how it all came together.

When the customer called him to deliver the good news, he learned his rivals had delivered recommendations that fell far short. And even more interestingly, he said this about the customer: "She [the customer] reluctantly let me know we won. I think it's because we behaved differently than anticipated. She expected us to be desperate and instead, had to treat us with respect." Success resulted not because their product was perfect or the cheapest but because they identified what made them unique and hammered it home with passion.

This triumph would change the trajectory of the company, as it was the most lucrative in their century-plus history. They had differentiated themselves and drove home how they were suited for this bid. And they rightfully, deservedly won.

Your role as leader is to transform your company from being "just another product or service" to being "in demand." When you're in demand, you act with confidence. If you're just "another" product, you'll display a low self-image and act with desperation—and as we know, desperate people (and the brands they lead) make desperate decisions. They lower prices, eliminate unique (but costly) product features, and imitate their competitors. As they do all this, their product quality plummets.

Why would anyone, including your leadership team, employees, suppliers, or sales network, be inspired to give their best to ensure the highest product or service quality to a brand that is soulless, rudderless, and in a "race to the bottom" in pricing?

Your competitors want you to act and think like this. Disappoint them! Procurement professionals beat up suppliers in the creative and service sectors just like they do their component and materials providers. It's all the same in their eyes. And they hope you eventually move over to their side. Don't buy into this.

Avoid "dumbing down" unique product features or streamlining processes to nothing but bare bones in your design or manufacturing. If that happens, the most powerful weapon in your battle to differentiate—your people—will lose faith. Employees making the product will lower their standards as the sales team representing the brand will negotiate against itself. All this, while your distribution system collectively rolls its eyes as a once proud brand deteriorates in front of them.

This happens with service providers as well.

A new client turned to me and declared, "I want my brand to be the Walmart of our industry." A surprising declaration since his company was a Christian-based insurance services organization whose primary customers were churches. A brand that was built on Christian principles now wanting to transform into a Walmart. Why?

The client shared his strategy: "There's a lot of profit in it if we go after the church business like our non-secular competition. We spend too much time, energy, and money doing all the extra things for the churches that the big guys would never do. Our current model is too costly for us to maintain. This new approach will save us tons of money and increase revenue."

The problem with his strategy was the brand had a wonderful niche: houses of worship. Their big, multi-national competitors didn't relate to churches like they did. And their pricing was premium, as they were 10–20 percent more expensive than the competition. I tried my best to influence the executive to reconsider, but he countered and replied, "We'll overcome any issues with the higher volume we'll get. That's why it's so important to become a Walmart."

Inside his company was malaise and unrest. As we interviewed executives and leaders, they expressed confusion over the company's direction. People were certainly not all on the same page. A familiar refrain we heard was, "We don't know what we want to be when we grow up." This is a popular rally cry in organizations that have not clearly identified their differentiation.

As my team prepared to interview and survey the company's customers, our client warned us. "We have a confounding customer base with all kinds of demographics. We can't make sense of it. One customer might be a small church with a wealthy, retired volunteer overseeing their insurance purchases. Other times, it's the job of the church secretary who is often at the low end of the salary spectrum. Sometimes it's the pastor buying our product. And at the mega-churches, the COO oversees it. It's a mess figuring out these people; they're so different."

While our client was accurate in describing the customers, he missed what was in front of him all along. He was just too close to see it.

His customers weren't so different, and there weren't four distinct customer profiles. There was *one*. Each customer was the *protector of their church*, regardless of their demographic. Their mindsets or *psychographics* were in lockstep: they cared about the church, keeping it safe, and preferred working with like-minded companies that felt the same about their faith. They turned to our client because his company proved that they would do whatever it took to help a house of worship succeed in their mission. His company's sales reps spoke the same language, quoted scripture, and in many cases attended the same churches as them. Customers were willing to pay more for that trusted relationship.

This revelation proved our client's brand had powerful differentiation as they were the trusted partner a church would turn to. We then created the slogan, *We Understand Why*. Three words, a "code," that would be deeply appreciated by every customer of theirs. Something their competition could never claim.

We revealed this to the leader. He paused and smiled. "This is what we've been searching for after spending decades trying to figure out who we really are." The search was over; it now made sense to everyone, and it was inspiring. The company's extra effort, the customer intimacy, all of that made them special and allowed them to command a premium. Their major competitors could not come close to replicating that. Instead of diminishing their brand, they now took pride in it.

We then conducted celebrations at their headquarters and branch locations and spread the word to every employee and representative, arming them to share the story and differentiation with customers, friends, and family. They all now *understood why.*

The malaise and confusion were gone as the dreams of being Walmart vanished. They now focused, with conviction, on being who they were.

Situations when Differentiation is Critical

⚡ **You plan to sell your company and want to increase its value.** Identifying your unique products and features can only add to the brand's cachet. For example, Apple has made it clear that it doesn't just manufacture MP3 players and computers; it positions itself as the technology giant that created the iPod, iPad, and iPhone. The value of that brand goes far beyond its assets.

⚡ **You feel it's hard to be all things to your customer base and want to simplify, yet intensify your focus.**

⚡ **You are the new leader who sees the business with clear eyes, and feels it provides far too much value without being compensated fairly.**

⚡ **You're considering significant investments in your facilities and equipment and need a more powerful brand identity that will support it.** CEOs often don't blink an eye at extraordinary capital investments in machinery or technology. Likewise, consider investing in your differentiation. It may yield a better return on investment (ROI) as it improves morale and employee performance.

⚡ **You strongly believe your team's engineering or manufacturing genius is not being appreciated or recognized by your customer base.** Time to make a statement that sets you apart.

⚡ **Your competitors are powerfully distinguishing themselves and taking market share from you.** It's time to counter that.

You'll find powerful and surprising results on this journey, and they can be felt enterprise-wide. Strong differentiation will also attract the best suppliers to the brand, inspiring them to run through walls to support you. Your customers will feel the same. And your employees will finally discover significance in what they do.

Do Employees View their Job as a Stepping-stone or a Destination?

How often I hear leaders state, "Our secret to success is our people!" I'll then ask, "So, you have a DNA advantage over your competitors?" And usually this is the response: "Well, our people are the best. Our clients love them. Our competition may claim the same, but our people are better."

Of course, your people are incredibly important, but that cliché is not enough—identify what makes them special. Is it expertise? Is it the level of training you provide them? Is it their years of experience that allows them to make on-the-spot decisions to better serve the customer? Once you discover how your people are unique, make that part of your culture, honor it, and reinforce it constantly.

In my company, we make it clear the top priorities (in this order) are taking care of our people, then serving our clients, and only after this, things like profitability and growth come into play. Internally, we constantly reinforce the message that we are here to help our clients (and their brands) look like heroes. *We are the people behind great people.* And to do that takes our entire team. Two loyal people who have been by my side for over twenty years focus on the top priorities. Patricia Love, Traffic Operations Manager, and Lori Jourdan, Finance Operations Manager, may not be well known to our clients, but they affect every relationship we have with them.

Patricia has championed our diversity efforts, inspiring our team to be inclusive and show sensitivity to all. She oversees "traffic" at the firm, which means ensuring the right person is on the right project for the right amount of time. That's not easy and it requires that our people also have time to recover after a project is completed.

Lori is a details-first advocate for us, making sure we do all the little things right. She ensures that we pay our suppliers on a timely basis, especially since many of them are small businesses or contractors. The same urgency applies to reimbursing expenses our employees incur on business travel. She also jumps in to do whatever it takes to help members on our team if they are momentarily overloaded with tasks.

Together, they transmit the message that we really do care, and in turn, clients feel that in the experience they receive, basing that on the countless times I've heard it said, "I love your team, they're amazing." In a creative firm like ours, despite them not being designers, writers, or account service managers, Patricia and Lori are every bit "rock stars."

From Why? *to* Wow!

A few years back, I wrote a business parable about how important employees are to the future of a company. In *From Why to Wow*, a good company transformed into an outstanding one because their team went from doubting their value to being amazed and proud at what they offered. People, all of us, need purpose, to know we do something of meaning. How can we feel true importance unless we represent something (a company or brand) that is unique? A great employee who assembles a product or provides a service she believes is mediocre is susceptible to moving on to another company that pays as little as twenty-five cents an hour more.

The role of the leader is to provide significance to every individual who represents or affects the enterprise. It's exhilarating to embrace what makes you unique and celebrate it with the most important people in the world, your employees. Take them from "why?" to "wow!"

Leaders differentiate. Now, let's meet our enemy, the "monster," *and* an inspiring company that defeated it!

CHAPTER 2

MEET THE COMMODITY MONSTER, BUT DON'T FEED IT!

IN CHAPTER ONE, WE SHARED compelling stories about celebrating differentiation and its value to an enterprise. The opposite is allowing your brand or product to be commoditized. Every day, you're in a battle with the Commodity Monster if you or your organization:

- ⚡ Think what you do is no different or no more valuable than what your competitors provide.
- ⚡ Offer a unique product, pay more to produce it, yet don't name it, promote it, or charge fairly for it.
- ⚡ Minimize or eliminate product features to lower your price.
- ⚡ Shift focus to unit sales, away from customer retention and profitability.

Companies large and small, private and public, all face this challenge. No matter if you compete globally or locally, you're in a battle against companies that have succumbed to the Commodity Monster. And if you jump in and act like them, you'll see your margins squeezed and profit depleted as you struggle to motivate your overworked, disillusioned organization.

This mindset stifles innovation, creativity, and inspiration—the very things that can free you from being a mere commodity. Business scholar and author Peter Drucker summed it up perfectly: "In a commodity market, you can only be as good as your dumbest competitor."[1]

Merriam-Webster defines a commodity as:

> com·mod·i·ty | \ kə-ˈmä-də-tē
> a good or service whose wide availability typically leads to smaller profit margins and diminishes the importance of factors (such as brand name) other than price.[2]

The above definition is demoralizing. It's your responsibility as a leader to forbid this message from becoming your mantra. Fight that battle! The opposite of a commodity is a differentiated brand. Let's change the description below into something inspiring:

> Your brand name
> a good or service that has unique characteristics, processes, and products that set it apart from its competitors, resulting in healthy profit margins, strong market share, proud workforce, and a powerful brand, enabling it to be in demand, purchased on its value and not on price alone.

Stand Up to the Commodity Monster

Our team was excited about working with an environmentally focused heating and air conditioning (HVAC) brand. Poised to grow, their brilliant product was geothermal—meaning it used the ground or water instead of electricity to produce warmth or cooling.

---

1   John Quelch, "When Your Product Becomes a Commodity," Harvard Business School, Working Knowledge Business Research for Business Leaders, last modified December 14, 2007, https://hbswk.hbs.edu/item/when-your-product-becomes-a-commodity.

2   Merriam-Webster, "Commodity," accessed August 16, 2023. https://www.merriam-webster.com/dictionary/commodity.

To fully understand the company and what it represented, my team conducted interviews with staff, dealers, and customers, culminating in a one-on-one with the president. An engaging, smart man, he was prepared and excited to talk about the business, its health, and product mix. I asked him for his "elevator pitch" or what he tells someone who approaches him with the question, "What does your company do?" His eyes lit up. "I get that all the time. I tell the person *we make HVAC systems.*"

I waited for him to complete his thought until it was clear that this was all he had to say. While hundreds of HVAC brands compete worldwide, very few are geothermal, yet his description of the brand was "We make HVAC systems."

This was also the message shared throughout the company and with customers and dealers as well. Their differentiation was being ignored and their margins, market share, and morale had been diminished. This company should have stood for far more than making HVAC systems: *they protected the environment through their geothermal innovations.*

Building on our confidence in their product and brand, my team spent days huddling with their engineers and designers, touring every inch of their manufacturing facility. We discovered several technologies that were extraordinary and earmarked them to be later named and promoted. We then created a logo, slogan, and marketing campaign that reinforced their environmental genius. Next, the leadership celebrated their differentiation with employees who had long been craving an inspiring message; the level of excitement was sky high.

Later that year, the company organized a dealer meeting where the leader and team unveiled the new brand, messaging, and vision for the future. Dealers were motivated; one stood up in front of the audience and said, "In my thirty years representing your company, this is the first time I've really been confident we're on the right track."

But the Commodity Monster attacked. And usually it is the leader who first succumbs. As my excited team left the convention hall after the dealer meeting, the president invited a few of us for drinks. As he lifted his whisky tonic, I was expecting a celebratory toast. Instead, he declared, "This dealer meeting has cost serious money and it's the last time we do anything like that." The president had calculated that the cost of rallying his employees and dealers around the brand was far too high and unsustainable. He wanted to return to a way of running the business that was far more comfortable.

The Commodity Monster had triumphed. This company, with all its incredible upside, would never come close to achieving its potential. It was a shame for the leader, its investors, employees, dealers, and customer base. A brand with amazing potential to help change our environment was reduced to merely being an "HVAC company."

How to Win the Battle Against the Commodity Monster:

- ⚡ **Starve it.** Resist treating your product or brand as a commodity; otherwise, it will become exactly that. You must differentiate your company from competitors and share its story with employees—from leadership to line workers. This inspires and engages everyone to be proud, produce a better product, and grow healthy relationships with customers.

- ⚡ **Develop a deep understanding of your customers; master their needs.** Learn from them. The more "human" they are to you, the more you'll realize they value, even love, what you are providing. Connecting with them gives you a chance to improve your offering. The commoditized competitors you compete against won't be wasting their time doing that. Take advantage. Build a loyal base of customers who can proudly explain why they chose you.

- ⚡ **Discover your uniqueness**. It may seem nothing sets you apart from a competitor. Have faith. Dig deep and unearth it. Could it be a process, a service, a piece of equipment, lean manufacturing, or brilliant design? Even if a competitor is doing something similar, but they aren't promoting it, you can be the first to "own" it. Take every opportunity to discover where your brand stands out. It's well worth the journey.

⚡ **Promote your people, not just your product.** No two companies have the same people on their team. Promote their experience, certifications, education—anything that sets you apart in the industry. Commodities don't have personalities or pride. Stand out from them as you *humanize* your brand and encourage your team. Kurt Breischaft, leader of COPPERWORKS (who I'll introduce you to shortly), highlights every employee on the company's website—over one hundred proud people with their photos and titles. You won't see a commodity do that.

⚡ **Capitalize on where you offer more.** Customers are often looking beyond just the product itself. Promote the additional value-added services and products you offer. For example, do you provide expertise and guidance to customers? Some companies boast a central location as an advantage; others have distribution networks that are exceptional at providing support and service. If you offer it, trumpet it.

⚡ **Never stop innovating or reimagining.** Is there a new product that would benefit your customers? Maybe you can bundle an extra service to provide value and convenience. Continued innovation can keep a product relevant and competitive in the marketplace. An inspiring culture of product reinvention sends the message that you are not just selling the same widget repeatedly; you're focused on improving and providing the customer with the ultimate product. *You care.*

Next, as promised, meet a leader who would not allow his brand to be commoditized.

Where Copper Works

Copper is a commodity listed on the London Metal Exchange (LME). Yet there is a copper rod producer that believed it offered something of great, unique value. Their president, Kurt Breischaft, told me, "We compete against mining operations where rod is not a priority to them, it's an afterthought. But we *love* making copper rod. Our engineers are experts at it. We need to stand out, or we'll be lost in a crowd of huge competitors selling cheap rod."

Kurt's company is a partnership between a domestic steel operation (SDI) and a 200-year-old Spanish metallurgy company (LaFarga) who christened it SDI LaFarga LLC. Their name had no individuality or personality. In addition, it confused customers, suppliers, employees, and the industry who referred to them by a host of names including SDI, LaFarga, those copper guys, scrap copper people, and other designations. Kurt was ready to change that discrepancy. "We need to find out who we are and claim our own identity."

My team toured their processing facility to discover what made them special, the key differentiators that would set the company apart from the competition. Collaborating with engineering leaders for days, we identified proprietary processes that allow the copper rod to be produced at an extraordinarily high-quality level while also being the most environmentally friendly process in the industry. That's quite a feat. Additionally, we learned that their customer experience was outstanding in comparison to the competition. It was commonplace for SDI LaFarga engineers to personally visit customer facilities and reconfigure machinery, helping them better process copper, a tremendous value-added service. No one else provided this.

The president was excited by what we were learning and said, "Next, we need to name this company. We must have our own identity!" This was bold because both "parents" were established, global success stories and most likely wouldn't be thrilled with their "creation" wanting to distance itself, no matter how positive the intent. Moving forward with Kurt and his leaders, my team conducted creative "jam" sessions to explore hundreds of possibilities. I didn't think a new name could or would be chosen, and I was wrong (and inspired by that).

Their search for differentiation was a triumph, a career highlight for many on the team as it gave birth to an inspiring identity: COPPERWORKS, as well as a new logo. We crafted an inspiring tagline celebrating their passion for copper and amazing work ethic: *This is where copper works*. Then, just as we were in the middle of developing the brand, the worldwide pandemic struck. Many companies were cutting back and waiting for the storm to clear, but that didn't deter Kurt.

He not only committed to continue rebranding the company, he also invested in the construction of a new furnace that would help them meet their anticipated future growth. Nothing could or would stop them as their brand's revitalization culminated in an internal employee launch.

The event was virtual, allowing for a safe celebration (due to the pandemic). All one hundred employees attended it via Zoom. To build the excitement, they were all sent a special launch package in advance. After logging in, they were instructed to open the package, finding their new logo on hats, mugs, and even on a craft beer. Kurt and the team shared the story behind their differentiation to reinforce how COPPERWORKS and their people were unique. Both parent companies joined the virtual celebration as well, cheering on the employees from across the globe.

Their new name, COPPERWORKS, is now proudly displayed across their 100,000-square-foot building, an inspiring billboard that can be seen a mile away. Kurt led the parade as the entire company joined in. And, after the launch, they posted the highest sales total in their history. They truly are where copper works.

Don't Fall Prey to the Commodity Mindset

Defeating the Commodity Monster takes discipline throughout an entire organization, from leadership to manufacturing to sales and everyone in between. When you consider the consequences of falling prey to the commodity mindset—diminishing profit, low morale, and inferior quality—it's well worth the time and investment. There must be something about what you do, your product, team, or processes, which makes you unique. If not, you'd no longer be in business.

Discover those differentiators, then promote them inside and outside your company to defeat the Commodity Monster for good. And, you don't have to be perfect in doing this, which I'll explain in the next chapter.

CHAPTER 3

DON'T GET CAUGHT IN THE "PERFECT TRAP"

"WE HAVE SO FAR TO GO, I'm exhausted thinking about it," Hank, a CEO at a cement mixer company confided. "Our mixers have decent features, but we aren't the best at anything and have our share of issues. My only hope is to get approval to increase the engineering budget, start designing a better product, and eventually capture market share. The problem is that this could take a long time, even years. Until then, we're stuck where we're at."

Hank was stuck, for sure, in what I call the "perfect trap." It's an obsession that tempts you to wait for the day when things are exactly right—and that day seldom, if ever, comes. It's just what the Commodity Monster and your competition want you to do: slow down and devalue your product until "perfect" comes along. As you pause, your brand is in a holding pattern.

Well-meaning leaders will pressure themselves and their teams to wait for that ideal time to "do it right." As a former songwriter, I learned that there is no such thing as perfection in the world of music. Countless hit songs were created *accidentally* when a performer placed their fingers in the "wrong" spot on the guitar or keyboard and that "mistake" was transformed into something magical. Perfect, in music, doesn't exist. It doesn't exist in the business world, either.

Imperfect yet magical situations take place in business, but companies often avoid them because they feel uncomfortable. See if this sounds familiar. Someone on your team proposes a great idea to promote your product to the world. Immediately, you and others feel the rush of adrenaline, but then fear creeps in. "Marketing will never go for that" or "We tried something like that years ago; it fell short" or other defeatist replies begin floating around the room until the idea is dropped. Paralysis then sets in as all progress slows to a glacial pace. Meanwhile, your competitors are moving at full speed.

If you hold back until everything is just right, by the time you launch your brand or product, almost everything has changed: the economy, the competition, your customers, even the world itself.

We're an American Band

The years I spent in rock bands enlightened me in many ways, including understanding that no one is perfect, and anyone, no matter their position, can contribute. Many of my bands' lead guitarists were brilliant soloists but merely so-so rhythm players. Some bandmates wrote songs. Others struggled at writing, but added their arrangement ideas to make our opuses more powerful. I worked with genius drummers who also were tremendous graphic artists, lending their talents to create band logos. Few of my bands had tremendous lead singers, most relied on vocal harmonies because none of us (me included) were blessed with extraordinary vocal range. While I wrote most of the material and sang a few songs, I had a more important role: showcasing the talents of each member to make us a better band.

I brought that same approach to running my company. My belief is that great ideas can come from anyone, not just the "creative department." Each person must be given support to make a positive difference by using their natural gifts. There is no "perfect" in my company. I'm not waiting for the ideal new employee to walk through our door. I'm searching for the best version of each person and giving that a chance to become reality.

Ship It!

Seth Godin published his journal on how to get things done, called *Ship It*.[3] I highly recommend it. He based it on Steve Jobs demanding his Apple engineers to meet deadlines by "shipping" products out the door and fixing the minor imperfections later. Jobs' team didn't initially receive it well because of their pursuit of perfection. He won out, as usual, and the product was soon "out the door." Today, we think nothing of receiving updates on our iPhones or *over the air* for our electric cars. These often include fixes for something that was imperfect in the previous version. If Jobs had allowed his team to wait until their programming was exactly right, there may never have been the iPhone or iPad. Instead, Apple grabbed a massive market share as it constantly updated its offerings.

Don't Let Perfection Derail Differentiation

Perfection obsession goes deeper than just the state of the product. It also sneaks into all areas of your potential differentiation.

Just as Apple's technology wasn't perfect when shipped, yet achieved great success, in my world of advertising, marketing, and training, no agency or firm is flawless. In fact, according to the site USBizdata.com, over 250,000 (256,541 to be exact) advertising agencies are in the U.S. In addition, over three million small businesses (employing five or fewer employees) and contractors practice advertising and marketing. That means my company competes against 16-billon-dollar revenue agencies (WPP and Omnicom) as well as the one-person "shop" down the street. Most of them will tell you they can help with your branding. So, how can I win the fight? I can't claim we will achieve results that are always superior to anyone else in the world, but I can offer up a differentiation that no one else has: *Brand Re-Engineering*™.

---

3   Seth Godin, " Do You Zoom, Inc.," filmed at the LinkedIn Hub Stage at Advertising Week XII, 2015, video, 10:28, https://www.youtube.com/watch?v=7YI1EtEMfgM.

Brand Re-Engineering is not just a name, it's our proprietary five-step brand discovery process. Of those five steps, almost all agencies offer two or three of them. But our company offers two that no one else does. Later, I'll share those steps, but in a world with millions of competitors, LABOV can't claim to be perfect, but we stand out due to our process.

This applies to all companies, including yours. For example, do you conduct a quality protocol in your plant that is unique? Does your customer service contain a step or options that few, if any, competitors offer? Notice, I didn't ask if your product was flawless or superior; that's usually up for debate. But if you can claim anything distinctive, tell the story.

The bigger the corporation, the more likely they are waiting for the ideal before a move is made. Larger companies tend to deal with more bureaucratic red tape, which means it takes longer to make decisions and act. They also have more moving parts, more departments, and more shareholders with sometimes conflicting motivations. All that interference and noise results in missed opportunities. That brings us to my next story of a worldwide brand that produced a product with a flaw but repositioned it as a differentiator.

No Glove Box

The late Alvin "Al" Swenson was a one-off. There will never be anyone like him. We met when he was a training manager for Volkswagen of America. He loudly introduced himself and shared his colorful life story. Prior to his position at VW, he was a football star at Yale, had raised horses, managed car dealerships, and was a trail guide. He was confident, dashing, irreverent, and smart. That personality also made him somewhat of a lightning rod. He attracted a small group of loyalists and an even larger group of detractors. He didn't play by the rules, which also made him fun to work with because he wanted to do things never done before.

He approached us to help make the new VW Passat launch a success. VW had gone through rough times, was experiencing low sales
and even lower *love* from the dealers that represented them. He guided
us into a secret garage at their U.S. headquarters to show us the new
Passat, and then issued a challenge. He said, "Look at this car. Go find
the problem; it's in there!"

My team conducted a Technical Immersion, first sitting down with
product experts and engineering teams, pouring through the vehicle.
As we were gleaning powerful insights on the product, and its features,
performance, and unique manufacturing processes, one very bizarre
flaw was uncovered. *The Passat did not have a glove box.* When we
shared this with Al, he beamed and said, "I see you found it. Now how
can we sell a car with no glove box?" He smiled wildly and asked, "Isn't
this exciting?" Like I said, he was one of a kind.

Al had a favorite saying, "You don't know what you don't know." (I
admit, it took me years to appreciate the brilliance behind those words.
At first, I thought it was a ridiculous statement.) This car was missing
a glove compartment for a good reason; we just *didn't know what we
didn't know.* Soon we learned the rest of the story.

Volkswagen's engineering team was well known for its obsession
with safety and innovative technology. In our discussions with them,
they told us the Passat was extraordinarily safe because it was designed
with "roll bars" to strengthen the vehicle's frame. These roll bars reinforced the car in the event of a head-on collision. They would encase
and protect passengers at impact instead of the much more common
situation of the engine being driven into the occupant area, which could
result in catastrophic injury or, worse, death. This was inspiring—a true
example of the highest safety standards. But then, the truth was revealed.

Unfortunately, Al explained, the VW engineers neglected to inform
their design team of this critical change to the interior of the vehicle.
The unit then proceeded straight into production, an ultra-safe vehicle
that happened to be missing a glove box. This issue was not addressed
until tens of thousands of them were on a boat from Germany destined

for the U.S., and ultimately to dealership lots.

We huddled with Al on how to truthfully and positively position this "imperfect" but otherwise well-made vehicle. We knew that if we didn't inform the dealer and customer as to why there was no glove box, they'd concoct their own assumptions (not flattering ones), because they *wouldn't know what they didn't know.*

Just as it was looking bleak, Al's amazing mind produced a brilliant golden nugget that changed everything. He said, "Gather 'round gang, we have a story to tell!" He continued as he reframed the issue. "It turns out that our beloved VW Passat is one of only two cars in the market that is missing a glove box. The other is a Mercedes-Benz, a super-luxury model that's priced at $200,000, eight times what our Passat costs!" His enthusiasm and genius were inspiring. True, the car was not perfect, but it was super-safe and had something in common with an uber-luxury car.

Now, instead of the message being "Here's a decent car with a defect," the message was, "We focus on advanced safety, so we've inserted roll bars in the car's front driver and passenger compartments, ensuring superior safety in a head-on collision. That means the Passat, like the $200,000 Mercedes-Benz super car, has no glove box."

Sure, there's a bit of spin to this, but truthfully, who cares if there's no glove box if we focus on a more important issue: this car is amazingly safe! We then helped train the hundreds of salespeople who represented VW nationwide to tell the story of the "missing glove box" with self-confidence. And as a nice touch, the brand ended up including a "trunk glove box" container in each Passat that made up for the omission. The model sold well, and when it was time for next year's version, guess what? It came with a glove box *and* roll bars in the front passenger compartments!

Al was viewed as a hero and soon left VW for . . . Mercedes-Benz. I should've guessed, but, then again, I didn't know what I didn't know!

Some of us don't like what we see in the looking glass. Our short-comings are revealed, and we believe others look not only different but better. That's in part why an estimated 1.4 million surgical and non-surgical facial plastic surgery procedures took place in 2022. Some people end up with numerous operations. Others are unhappy, often trying to reverse the results after realizing that they would have been better off leaving things naturally. Next up is the story of a wonderful brand that looked in the mirror and went under the knife to look more like their competitors. Fortunately, they were able to revert to looking like themselves.

Look in the Mirror

Newmar RV, headquartered in Nappanee, Indiana, is a highly respected Amish recreational vehicle brand known for exacting craftsmanship and customization. For years, they enjoyed great success manufacturing luxury recreational vehicles that were bespoke, offering so many options to customers that it was astounding. You could choose any appliance or fabric. Or design your own floorplan. Nothing was off limits.

Customers craved the chance to create their own Newmar masterpiece. Of course, offering all this came at a cost for the brand and dealers as it was complex, time-consuming, and low-profit work. Dealers complained that it took hours of navigating through all the customer whims while Newmar's manufacturing leaders felt it too demanding to constantly change production lines and reposition machinery to build models with unique specs, floorplans, and furniture. It was a challenge they endured since Newmar was all about customization.

Then the leadership decided to adopt the approach of much larger competitors such as Winnebago, the larger, high-quality brand that offered significantly fewer options. "Winnie's" customers were satisfied with a well-made, but less customized RV that was also easier for the manufacturer to produce and the dealer to sell.

Newmar announced they would no longer offer a fully customized RV to customers, and instead, move forward offering an excellent unit with far fewer options. The dealers would no longer have to endure the laborious, time-consuming hassle. Initially, the results were fantastic, with higher profit and far less complexity. The product, while less unique and certainly not customized, was a breeze to sell and build, but now a Newmar RV would look and be equipped pretty much like every other RV.

Slowly—within six months—sales dried up as customers bought rival coaches. Dealers grew frustrated as Newmar was no longer that special brand; it was a look-alike, a "me-too." Despite the initial financial improvement, it became clear that Newmar was now competing head-to-head with bigger brands that knew how to mass produce and mass market far more successfully than they did. The brand was losing their position in the market and had to do something fast.

After months of disappointing sales, management wisely decided to reinstitute customization. Dealers and customers were happy they were going back to their roots. Newmar had lost numerous customers during this experiment, but over time, and with much effort, they gradually won many of them back to the brand.

This story has many facets to it. Kudos to their leaders for quickly adapting after realizing they erred. It was a calculated move that did not work out but was a learning opportunity for all involved. At its heart, Newmar was the customizable luxury RV. Instead of trying to compete against cookie-cutter products at a similar price point, they now proudly discovered that they were worth more and (drum roll…) charged for it. Valuing their differentiation resulted in far higher profit, morale in the plant, and robust sales at the dealership. Newmar now identified who they were and maximized it.

A Champion for Going Beyond

James Meyer has been a respected leader in the automotive, recreational vehicle (RV), and railway industries for decades. He's a trusted friend to my company and me. With his brilliant engineering and product development mind, Jim, on numerous occasions, has courageously demanded that the quality of his product is either excellent or it will not leave the plant.

I collaborated with him on the launch of a port truck, which is a heavy-duty vehicle used to transport containers or freight over short distances. They are not glamorous products; they are workhorses. This launch was critical to the future of the brand and there was intense pressure to deliver on an aggressive production schedule to meet pent-up demand. While the truck was designed with ingenious features and no doubt had great potential, it had to be incredibly durable to meet the grueling demands placed on it every day. That's where Jim put his foot down.

Much to the dismay of many on his team, he required the unit be tested to its limits at a proving ground and until it passed muster, he would not allow the launch to proceed. His rationale was sound: since the truck was positioned as virtually indestructible, it had to achieve arduous performance standards, or it was a no-go. The launch inevitably was delayed, and dealers were irritated (as were some on Jim's team). But after incredible tenacity and rigor, it did pass and was released successfully.

It may have been frustrating to some, but Jim's position made it clear to all in his organization that quality is king. While he understood no product is perfect, he ensured that his team was proud of what was being delivered to the customer. That's become a personal differentiation for him and every brand he's touched.

Swede Success

Jonas Dahlen, a distinguished and influential sales executive in the healthcare sector, has established himself as a leader over the course of decades. Born in Sweden and now a U.S. citizen, he refused to adopt the common approach of using forceful tactics and pressure to manage sales teams. Jonas has attained success by demonstrating respect toward his team members. He realizes that perfection is not attainable and shares his belief in treating people in a manner that would inspire him personally. While he is not one to compromise on performance, he sets clear, achievable expectations for each individual. Jonas firmly believes that combining respect with transparent communication regarding expectations is the most effective approach.

Progress, Not Perfection

It's not about being perfect, it's all about making progress. Companies throughout the world have experienced situations that have temporarily drained them of their character and value. See if any of these scenarios sound familiar:

You Got Older and Lost Passion

Come on, shouldn't it make sense to be proud of a brand that has been in business for forty or even two hundred years? Unfortunately, this is seldom how leaders and organizations look at themselves, as time slowly erodes and tests their passion and confidence. An established company must never lose sight of why it was successful in the very beginning. It also must reinvent itself as the world around it changes. And, truthfully, most companies that have been around awhile do neither. Be that rare company.

You're Playing Too Safe

Good old grandpa Harry was an amazing guy. He was always creating innovative ideas and hanging out with customers, making promises that were almost impossible to keep, but, somehow, he did. Organizations founded on great passion and energy, as generations come and go, will lose all that if the current-day motivation for its leaders is protecting their position or country club membership. Grandpa, when he started, had little to lose. Decades later, these leaders feel *everything* is at risk. You don't need to be reckless to regain your differentiation, but you must step up, be bold, and lead again.

Meet the New Boss, Same as the Old Boss

The executive turnstile will see companies erasing their previous initiatives, only to replace them with new ones in the next regime. A casualty of these changes is your differentiation because no one owns it anymore. Don't let that happen. While some may view it as a relic of the past, revisit it and allow it to reclaim its deserved greatness.

Your Brands Became Homogenized

Maybe you're the leader of a company that has acquired many other brands in the segment. There is probably a strong temptation to "streamline" them, transforming those formerly unique companies into boring, mediocre, one-size-fits-all brands that no longer have their own personality or value. Here's an example with the names changed to protect the innocent:

A truck manufacturer (I'll call them TriState Trucks) did just this and, at one point, purchased ten companies in its segment. Immediately, they consolidated their manufacturing to only three plants to economize and reduce the workforce. TriState then positioned their brands as virtually the same as each other, cutting their marketing budget. And their once separate, competitive dealer networks even started to comingle, leaving some brands to wither away. It looked logical to do but was disastrous. They soon learned, if you own many brands, they each need their own "lanes to swim in." They turned to us for help.

I sent in our Technical Immersion Group to tour their largest facility and identify any potential specialty in features, technology, or processes. Several of their brands were manufactured there, on the same line by the same team. Tony, their Marketing VP, proudly guided us to a beautiful truck and said, "I want to show you our flagship brand first. Let's start at the top so you can see us at our very best." As he was proudly demonstrating its features, he halted in mid-sentence and uttered an expletive. Turning to us, he confessed. "Sorry, this isn't our flagship truck. It's actually our entry-level brand. They all look so much alike."

Here we were with the leader of manufacturing, and he couldn't tell his premium brand from the lowest-level product. You can be sure that neither could his customers or dealers. This issue blurred the lines between brands. Their flagship marque, mid-range, and entry-level offerings lost their identities and value. It took months of concerted effort to remedy the situation as we identified and promoted each brand's specific position in the portfolio, as they now had their own lane to swim in.

In this scenario, focus was on efficiency to the point that it snuffed out differentiation and character. You simply cannot "dumb down" unique product features. An organization will fail as it gives into that temptation by rounding out a product's "sharp edges." Premium brands that create a lower-priced offering as a "line extension" often find this effort results in deteriorating the value of the entire brand. It comes down to honoring your unique value instead of creeping closer to a commodity in the hopes of gaining profitless market share.

Where's Your Focus?

I often encounter companies that take scientific approaches, measuring inputs and outputs, and following strict criteria to achieve agreed-upon goals. That's great, though it's not the only way to run an enterprise. Your differentiation may not seem logical or result in measurements that support its existence. But then again, how can you measure the *Mona Lisa*? Is country music better than jazz? Are Macs better than

PCs? View your brand in the same fashion. There is room for science and art in the search for differentiation.

In my career, I've encountered far too many companies that were internally focused. It's tempting for even the best to forget it's not about them or about making things easy as they "endure" their irritating customer base or demanding sales channel. When it becomes all about us, relationships suffer and so do our brands and differentiation.

A never-ending search to increase margin by another percent may eventually erode market share. One department competing against another over how much they contribute can take focus away from the overall value you're providing. The customer doesn't know or care what division makes more profit and they rarely distinguish between the performance of the manufacturer and the distribution channel. Focus on how to uniquely serve the customer, not on how your enterprise serves itself.

There are many ways a brand can become uninteresting, uninspiring, and undifferentiated. The critical point to remember is that these factors challenge all companies at some point. A leader must constantly make sure the brand, its differentiation, and the story behind it are all relevant, inspiring, and interesting, despite being imperfect. Never fall into the "perfect trap."

Be prepared, there will be moments of discomfort as you travel through this discovery. Give it time. Just like that song you first heard and didn't like but then grew on you until it became a favorite, it may take a little time to fall in love with your differentiation—but once you do, you'll be singing its tune.

CHAPTER 4

BEST-KEPT SECRETS, ME-TOOS, AND SLEEPING GIANTS

I'VE OFTEN WORKED WITH BRANDS that described themselves as a best-kept secret, a "me-too" imitator, an old, groggy "sleeping giant," or other less-than-inspiring terms. As a leader, challenge and eliminate those labels or they will grow stronger within the walls of your company, defining and restricting you.

Best-Kept Secret: Not Good Unless You're a Spy

The late Virgil Miller, a wonderful, inspiring Amishman, oversaw the luxury recreational vehicle (RV) maker, Newmar RV. In our first meeting, he beamed with pride, "All of us here are so proud of our RVs. We like to say we're the best-kept secret in the industry." I respectfully challenged his point of view. "If your brand is a best-kept secret, that means you're investing money and resources building something amazing but are neglecting to share that good news." He responded, "Well, we don't brag. It's against our culture."

Virgil was certainly a humble man. Originally studying to be a minister, he was called to lead this successful manufacturer. Daily, employees would approach him to discuss their lives and, sometimes, their struggles, asking for his valued guidance. In reality, he was the "minister" of the company. He also became a spiritual mentor for me as I had the privilege to work with and learn from him for many years. Virgil, while being an understated man, was surprisingly entertaining. Once, I called him to check in and asked what he was doing. He chuckled. "I'm looking out the window at some SOBs." I was surprised, because I had never heard him say anything off-color before and asked, "What's an SOB?" He replied with a smile. "Barry, SOB stands for 'some other brand.' There's a gravel lot across the street with our competitors' units parked there. I was taking a look at them." Another time he entertained me was shortly after a serious winter snowstorm hit our region. He informed me that a couple of his employees called in to tell him they had no power at their house and couldn't make it into work. I said, "So what?" He laughed and said, "Come on, I knew they were joking because they were Amish and never had electricity at their house." Virgil told them, "Very funny, now get in your buggy and go into work!"

Virgil, in addition to being engaging, had an engineering mind. My father, an electrical engineer, was always the smartest person in the room when I was growing up. Engineers, however, while brilliant, often dismiss the need to communicate the uniqueness of their inventions, because they assume everyone knows. Truth is, nobody knows or cares about an innovation unless you show them why they should.

Over the course of my career, I've met and collaborated with brilliant engineers like Virgil. Many have told me that they feel their company's salesforce is costly and unnecessary, as the product should sell itself. I've tried to counter that argument by convincing them to train their sales team to demonstrate the brand's innovations with customers. When accomplished, your product will command a premium, and customer retention will be strong. Conversely, an untrained sales network that sees little value or differentiation in their brand will be a detriment, merely selling "stuff" at whatever price they can get.

If you feel your brand is a best-kept secret, it's time to identify its differentiation, and equally important, communicate and celebrate it to the world. By the way, the founder of Newmar RV, Mahlon Miller, is also a devout and amusing Amishman. Each year, he'd address the dealers at their annual meeting and perform his version of an Amish stand-up comedy routine, entertaining them with funny quips. Here's a joke shared by him: *Do you want to know how to make sure you have some beer left for yourself when you go fishing with an Amishman? Invite two Amishmen.*

Me-Too: Imitation Is Not Flattering

Here's how to know if you're a "me-too" company: Are you in second, third, or fourth place in your segment? Were you founded by a smart person who focused on a top competitor and made a cheaper version of that product? Is your enterprise satisfied with being in second or third place? A me-too brand is just inches away from a commodity, and if leaders don't correct course, they'll forever remain a lower-volume, low-priced brand lacking in customer or employee loyalty.

The key is to show respect to your brand by discovering what it does that makes it the choice of your best customers. Customers rarely have to buy from you, so learn why they choose you. And as that exploration deepens, glean from your sales network what has allowed this brand to survive, ignoring, of course, the standard answer of a lower price.

Scott Lord, a long-time leader in the trucking industry, approached us to help him reinvigorate his brand. The company had long been known as the number two truck in its segment. We collaborated with him to launch a brand-new model destined to replace its highest-selling unit. Determined to break the me-too spell, Scott met resistance throughout the company. Surprisingly, even some of his engineers were lackadaisical about the new product. Wisely, he realized it was a lot to expect of people who for decades had "me-too brand" tattooed on their psyche.

We conducted a Technical Immersion, diving deep into their manufacturing, design, and engineering. Brilliant features and components were uncovered, such as the military-grade steel, imported from Sweden, used to build the frame rails. The brand's trucks also boasted industry-first features that made them easier to service. As the differentiation story of the truck was built, so was the enthusiasm and belief that Scott's team began to feel in the product. The entire enterprise went from "why" (why are we wasting time on this?) to "wow" (I can't believe how impressive this product is).

The truck was a game changer in the industry, representing the best of what made his brand unique. Employees were so excited that they repainted the plant before celebrating with the dealers as the first truck rolled off the line. With pride, Scott's sales team shared the story of every unique material, every impressive innovation, and each smart customer-centric design embodied within this truck. The energy was amazing; the support was strong; this brand was no longer a "me-too."

The product launched, but, shortly after, the company underwent organizational changes that temporarily set them back, as Scott and others exited. A half decade later, the company refocused and began seeing considerable, impressive progress. It's not just about a product— you need people (starting with leaders like Scott Lord) who believe they represent far more than just a me-too brand.

Sleeping Giants: Time to Poke the Bear

Many formerly dominant brands have lost momentum over their years of existence. The primary cause of this malaise, surprisingly, is success. Decades of success can slowly demotivate entire enterprises as they "play it safe," protecting their position. This inevitably results in less aggressiveness, investment, and risk-taking as that powerhouse devolves into a very large, slow-moving cream puff.

Sleeping giants were often trailblazers and the originators of their segment. Despite this legacy, their products, plants, and facilities grew tired and stale. Leaders of sleeping giants often tell us they feel they are hanging on the ledge by their fingernails, fearful of what the future holds.

These brands usually have a wealth of differentiation that they can recultivate and revitalize. Their founding principles may have become clouded and dusty, but still influence the company today. The amazing products developed in the past are still talked about glowingly, but too often the company has watered them down or, worse, discontinued them. They can be reborn.

The competition is keenly aware of the sleeping giant's potential and is cautious not to awaken it because these brands will often have maintained some of the strongest dealers and customers. All this upside, yet the company is floundering.

When asked to revitalize a sleeping giant, we first interview their loyal dealers, customers, and employees to discover their passion for the brand, plus learn of the ideas they wish the company were pursuing today. Dealers and suppliers will share a sense of family when speaking of their long history with the brand. We then dig into the technical capabilities and processes and will undoubtedly find nuggets of gold (differentiators) that have been in front of the team for years. Now is the time for leaders to leverage all that intellectual property, value, and differentiation to enable the brand to be formidable once more (and even better, to irritate the competition).

It will inspire the entire enterprise to witness this rebirth. Time to wake up the giant.

Awakening an RV Icon

John Draheim is an automotive and recreational vehicle executive with an advanced, analytical mind. He elevated many brands, using his talents, including a sleeping giant. When he took the helm at an established recreational vehicle brand, he faced a dealer revolt as many of them had become estranged due to their relationship with former ownership. John pledged to be a true partner, welcoming them back and assisting many financially. He then revitalized the formerly dominant company with new passion and a fresh, industry-leading product line-up. Applying his automotive experience, he instituted a revolutionary manufacturing process that transformed the brand, separating it from the pack.

John would not allow his company to rest on its former glory, which, in turn, re-energized employees and dealers to dedicate their efforts toward seeing this once proud brand reach the pinnacle again.

Nicknames to Steer Clear of

Another modifier that many people use in describing their companies is the word "just." Just a local manufacturer, just another jet charter service, or just another assembler of wire harnesses for the RV industry. *Yawn.* Never allow yourself to be a "just" brand. Your child is not "just" a kid; your child has a name.

Outlaw all terms that diminish your brand efforts. Create an awareness that we aren't "another" or "just" or a "local" whatever. Pay attention to how employees, dealers, customers, and competitors describe your company or brand. Listen closely—do terms like "best-kept secret" or "sleeping giant" feel good when you hear them? Would a person referring to you in that way mean it positively? Of course not.

Not Just Another Patient...or Doctor

Garry V. Walker, MD, is a leading anesthesiologist and author. Dr. Walker makes it a point to view every patient as a unique individual. "I find it my purpose to provide validation to each person I treat, no matter if she is a five-year-old undergoing a dental procedure or an octogenarian recovering from hip surgery. Each person has a story, a need, and deserves total focus from me. The patient isn't an interruption in my day, they *are* my day." Garry doesn't view someone as "just" the next patient, which is why he is never referred to as *just* an anesthesiologist.

Think about your favorite products and brands. How do you describe them and with what emotion? We must want our customers to do the same regarding us. It's time to retire unhealthy terms that diminish the value of your company and brand.

CHAPTER 5

LEARNING FROM CENTURY-OLD COMPANIES

"OUR PRODUCT IS MEDIOCRE, even worse than in the past. Facilities are dirty, and morale is low. Our leadership team puts the 'fun' in dysfunctional; it's a mess. On top of all of this, we can't keep up with demand and are losing money." Quotes like this one are too common in today's business world. What might make it surprising is that it originated from the CFO of a food manufacturer that was established over 120 years ago.

This is a company that has endured and thrived for over a century, yet one of its leaders viewed it with a sense of embarrassment. No doubt he felt this way because he cared so deeply. It's sad, but we tend to view our brands with less "love" as time goes on.

Let's consider the above company. At the time, the CFO referenced the pandemic and the challenge of dealing with it, as well. When I heard this, I interjected. "Isn't it interesting that this is not your company's *first* pandemic? Your company has survived two global epidemics, two world wars, the Great Depression, recessions, and somehow this disappointing company is in demand." The leader paused and reconsidered. "Hmmm, we aren't a complete failure, maybe we do something right." He was correct. Even though his company needed to revitalize their brand, they had enormous potential.

That day, we began a two-year journey re-energizing that brand. My team toured their facilities and spoke with engineers, product experts, and employees working on the plant floor to identify differentiators that could be promoted. There we learned of the extraordinary processes they had devised to ensure the highest product quality. Those needed to be spotlighted. We interviewed their customers and learned of deep, meaningful relationships cultivated over the years. This led to us helping them refine and name their own "experience" that only they offered. Along this journey of brand renewal, hundreds of employees were interviewed in-person or through surveys to get their input. Everyone was offered a chance for their voice to be heard.

We took the learnings and developed brand messaging, visuals, and support materials that reinforced what made this centenarian company so extraordinary.

The culmination of this effort was an employee celebration event at all locations to thank them for their contributions and share the relaunching of the company and brand. Hundreds of dedicated people went from viewing their company with embarrassment to feeling proud and truly engaged.

You might say, "Sure, this sounds great, but what about the fact they weren't making a profit? All the warm and fuzzy stuff is nice, but show me the money!" That is a fair question. Here's the answer. Prior to our working with the company, leaders felt they were "lucky" to have any business at all and feared even minor price increases would surely result in lost customers. As their belief in themselves and differentiation grew, so did their confidence. More each day, they became convinced they were providing a product and experience of great value and slowly began charging for it, successfully. Sales rose, profits jumped, and employee retention reached an all-time high.

A Recipe for Longevity

Take a moment to add up the few companies you know that have been around for 50 years. Now, think of the brands that are over one century old. It's a short list. That's because 96 percent of businesses fail in their first 10 years[4]. Fewer survive three decades, and almost none are alive a century later. It's a rare distinction and something to be proud of.

Over the years, my firm has worked with dozens of companies that have reached this stratum. There's much to learn from resilient brands that have weathered the storms for a century or more and came out on top. These nine insights apply to a 120-year-old brand as well as a start-up.

1. It's Personal

The best companies care, even after a century. To them, it is personal; their product, quality, and relationships matter to them deeply. That sense of ownership and dedication permeates the great ones long after the founder has passed the baton. Their leaders feel the responsibility to continue what the company has stood for and "don't want to mess this up."

2. Deep Connection with Product or Service

The great ones not only created their brand, but they continue to "live" it. They consume it, experience it, and understand it better than anyone. It's not just a brand or product, it's "us." Whether it's beer, Scotch, motorcycles, cars, trailers, trucks, components, or jet services, the leaders—and often the entire enterprise—are consumers of, and ambassadors for, the brand.

Garrett Finney, founder of TAXA Outdoors, a start-up camper trailer manufacturer out of Houston, Texas, is a brilliant architect who has consulted with organizations worldwide, including NASA. While there, he designed parts of the International Space Station and also consulted on lunar habitats capable of sustaining humans in extreme conditions. Equally important, he is an outdoor enthusiast.

---

4   Bill Carmody, "Why 96 Percent of Businesses Fail Within 10 Years," Inc., August 12, 2015.

All of this has led Garrett and the team to create TAXA's other-worldly habitats filled with ingenious features for camping and over-land experiences—adventure equipment you can sleep in. That instinct for designing mobile spaces and passion for the outdoors allow TAXA to stand out against its competition, giving them the best chance to succeed long-term.

3. Constant Reinvention

One thing you'll see from companies that have been in business for over a century is they've continued to develop. That might mean realigning products or services to keep them relevant as the world changes. It can also be a complete reinvention. Look at Procter and Gamble (P&G). They began as a soap and candle company in 1837. Today, P&G owns a raft of iconic brands, from toothpaste to detergent.

On the opposite end of the spectrum is Kodak, once a giant in the photography industry. It failed to reinvent itself when digital imagery disrupted the market. What's even more astonishing is that one of Kodak's own engineers invented the first digital camera in 1975. Kodak could have remained a leader in the industry but failed to adapt to a changing market.

Founded over 120 years ago, FreightCar America once held the mantle as the nation's premier manufacturer of coal railcars. However, with the decline of coal mining, the company's prominence in the rail industry began to wane. Faced with a multitude of unused railcars scattered across freight yards nationwide, FreightCar was compelled to reimagine its products in order to remain viable.

Under the leadership of Jim Meyer, Chairman, and his team, including Greg Josephson, Vice President of Engineering, and Matthew Tonn, Chief Commercial Officer, FreightCar embarked on a remarkable journey of transformation. In late 2019, they identified an emerging opportunity: the conversion of small cube hopper cars. These seemingly insignificant coal railcars became a foundation of FreightCar's reinvention.

Over the course of several years, the company undertook the ambitious task of converting more than 1,000 of these small cube "donor cars" into modern designs. This feat not only breathed new life into the aging railcars but also showed FreightCar's adaptability and innovation. In doing so, this century-old company, originally rooted in the coal industry, positioned itself as an environmental and sustainability leader.

4. Customers are Sacred

To surpass the century mark and thrive beyond it, exceptional companies develop a deep connection with their end-users, treating them as an extension of the brand and an invaluable source of unofficial research and development. These companies genuinely adore their customers, embracing their quirks and differences without reservation because they are considered part of the family.

The visionary leaders of these immensely successful companies actively seek input from end-users to enhance their offerings, often sharing in the brand experience together. Whether the product is a motorcycle or a fire truck, they happily join bike owners on cross-country motorcycle rides or proudly stand shoulder to shoulder with customers as fellow volunteer firefighters battling the flames. By immersing themselves in these experiences together, new ideas are born as they forge an unbreakable bond.

5. Unceasing Innovation

Harley-Davidson got its start in 1903 when four industrious young men secured a small engine onto a bicycle. Had they stopped there, they wouldn't have gotten very far, literally or figuratively. Over the years, their engines grew more powerful, their motorcycles more sophisticated and technological. Today, Harley-Davidson is among the most iconic brands in the world. One of the company's leadership principles is "agility—accelerating, innovating, and thriving in a rapidly changing environment." That direction is evident in the brand's first electric (EV) motorcycle, the LiveWire®. It represents the motor company's continued drive to transform its product offering. Longtime brands realize even greater success when they focus on what makes them unique and then make it relevant in today's world.

Universal Studios in Burbank, California, was founded in 1912. In the 1930s, as the Great Depression threatened to shutter their operations, they decided to focus on a particular genre, *horror movies*. For the next decade, their classics included *Frankenstein*, *The Mummy*, *Dracula, The Invisible Man*, and dozens of others. Those motion pictures, for their time, were so convincing, medical crews were dispatched to theaters to care for the throngs of fainting patrons. Universal, due to this decision, was reinvigorated and has thrived to this day.

6. Mastery of the Experience

The best centenarians are *maestros* in the art and science of the brand experience. Every year, The Macallan Scotch whisky brand conducts hundreds of luxurious consumer events to share the story and incomparable taste of its whisky. This two-century-old brand believes there is no better way to fall in love with The Macallan and its people. The energy, the pride, and the genius of your brand are best revealed through the experience you deliver.

Harley-Davidson understands the power of their customer experience. The Harley Owners Group, or HOG, represents over a million Harley-Davidson owners in over ninety countries worldwide. Bruce Motta, HOG Regional Manager, has led the HOG Officer Training program for years as his team has inspired and trained thousands of regular folks like you or me to represent the brand at their local dealerships. These impassioned "officers" organize HOG events and experiences, including national, regional, and touring rallies, group rides, and get-togethers, as well as anniversary celebrations in Milwaukee, Wisconsin, home of Harley-Davidson. Member activities are organized the whole year through, even during the winter when owners put their motorcycles away. These off-season events keep the connection to the brand alive even when it's "out of sight." As a premier lifestyle brand,

Harley-Davidson is fueling the passion of its owner base by encouraging them to interact with each other and the brand as often as possible. Bruce fuels this passion that deepens the commitment of their riders to the motor company. From Prague to Gainesville, HOG is keeping the thunder of the brand alive.

7. Nurturing Relationships Beyond the Customer

A product is only as good as the pieces and parts that go into it. Any 100+-year-old enterprise will tell you that establishing strong supplier and sales channel relationships is key to their success. The best will foster extraordinarily close, honest, and trusted relationships that transcend the transactional.

One manufacturer we work with has fostered enduring relationships with suppliers and dealers, some of which have lasted a century. They've instilled into their culture a commitment to tirelessly work with dealers to ensure they are satisfied with every aspect of the product before the customer takes delivery. If that means dispatching a service team on a weekend to fix an issue, so be it. Their suppliers, likewise, have a devoted relationship with them as well, whether it be in co-designing a new feature or in streamlining how they do business together. This emphasis on relationships reaps dividends for all concerned, including their loyal customers, who for over a century have benefited from this as well.

8. Legacy Relevance

These century-plus success stories don't live in the past, they build on it, using who they were on Day One to help guide and inform them where to go next. They hold tight to the entrepreneurship or the engineering process that catapulted their success and reinforce that story throughout the enterprise. No one else has that differentiation. Why forsake it?

Rick Brown, Chief Customer Officer of Aunt Millie's Bakeries, which was founded in 1901 and is still led by the Popp family, realized this bakery has always been committed to being the best value in the bread aisle. Their top competitors, which are mega-corporations, can't make that claim. This brilliantly sets Aunt Millie's apart as *the family bakery that values family*. This distinction was authentically theirs, and the competition could not counter it.

And, to top it off, we applied the idea of "value" to the company's employees, launching a campaign celebrating them as the brand's "special ingredient" on billboards located across the Midwest (positioned near their bakeries). Each featured Aunt Millie's employees, along with their job titles and signatures with the headline, *Our Special Ingredient is Our People*. VP Bohn Popp proclaimed it as "the best program in our history." Placing the billboards near their plant locations was a great motivator for the employees and helped attract the attention of their families, communities, and potential new hires as well.

9. Sense of Community

Centenarians support their community as well, often being the marquee business in their area. These brands are the greatest of givers, yet they usually underplay it. And they consider their employees as family, committed to providing them with a stable, proud work environment.

Betts Industries of Warren, Pennsylvania, is part of the fabric of their community. Spanning over 120 years, the Betts family has withstood pandemics, world wars, and economic challenges to ensure people are taken care of in their community. Through their various sponsorships and charitable contributions, the family has remained a beacon of hope and an employment destination for thousands in their region.

I remember Cathy Schannen, LABOV VP, calling me late one night, inviting me to join her in a heartfelt midnight discussion with the Betts family during the COVID-19 pandemic. The Betts executive team, led by Charles "Chad" Betts, President, was battling an impending governmental regulation that threatened to temporarily shutter the plant. The concern for Chad and VP of Marketing and Business Development, Michelle Betts, wasn't loss of revenue; it was all about the well-being of their employees and families. Their customers joined the effort and rallied behind them, assisting in providing the documents required to prove that the Betts operation was in fact "essential." In short order, they were among the first wave of companies allowed to re-open, inviting the employees back. This focus on doing the right thing for the right reasons prompted my team to create Betts' slogan, *Do What's Best*. Since 1901, the Betts family has done just that.

I have nothing but admiration and respect for those companies that have survived and thrived for a century or more. They've achieved where so many have failed. Building on their past experiences, successes, challenges, and passion, they continue to journey forward as leaders in their respective industries. Whether a company has survived two pandemics or is a start-up, we can apply learnings from these trailblazers as we strive to be counted among their ranks in the future.

CHAPTER 6

NAME IT AND OWN IT

COMMODITY OR COPYCAT PRODUCTS RARELY HAVE NAMES, or at least interesting, original ones. Once you identify your brand's differentiators, give them their own identities, rewarding them with the attention and respect they deserve.

During an assessment of an aviation brand, I was surprised that their jets did not display their logo. To complicate things even more, each of their models had its own name, in many cases, with no connection to others in the line-up. This was a well-known company that produced and engineered excellent products yet disregarded their identity.

I turned to the CEO to learn the reasoning behind all this. He replied, "As for why we named our models what we did, it was really something that just happened over time. We have no naming convention or hierarchy."

When I pressed him on his jets neglecting to feature the brand logo, he sighed, "That's something I've wondered about as well. I'll sit on the tarmac and see a plane ahead of me and wonder if it's one of ours." He explained how this came about, "Around ten years ago, a customer asked us to paint their company's logo on his jet and, in doing that, we removed ours. Our manufacturing team then recommended we save the extra time and effort on our planes moving forward by leaving off our logo. It was a cost-cutting move." In reality, it was a *brand-cutting move.*

A new jet can cost from two million to over a hundred million dollars. Its image and reputation are critical, yet this manufacturer *erased* their identity because, in the past, one customer wanted their own logo on his aircraft. That decision, along with their confusing model names, diminished the manufacturer's value for decades. Your brand's name and logo matter.

Better than Used

Luxury automakers Mercedes-Benz and Lexus introduced a breakthrough in the early 1990s. They transformed the concept of a used vehicle, differentiated it, and bestowed upon it a special name, *Certified Pre-Owned* (CPO). The genius behind this was that, until then, only car dealers benefited from the sale of used autos on their lot. Some used cars were "clunkers," others may have been in pristine condition, but they all were known as merely *used cars.* Until CPO.

CPO was the best of all worlds. Despite it having a previous owner, an auto being certified as CPO ensured it was in top shape, with worn-out parts replaced, and all safety issues were addressed and fixed by the dealer during inspection. It also came with a warranty that was nearly as good as a new car's. Basically, you were buying a used model that was almost new for far less. It was not merely a used car; it was Certified Pre-Owned and had premium value. Sure, that distinction cost the customer a grand or so more, but it was worth it. By naming this unique offering, even more cache, or value, was created for both the dealer and the brand.

And like with most great innovations, everyone won. The customer purchases a car they can trust. The dealer earns more profit from CPO than new unit sales because they are reimbursed by the brand for the inspection plus charge a premium to the customer. And the auto manufacturer wins because CPO vehicles have been proven to increase resale prices, which builds their brand value.

Great concepts can take time to catch on. Meeting with leaders at Kia Motors a decade after CPO was first created, I asked them about their approach to it, only to hear one of the executives ask, "What's a CPO?" In the early 2000s my team was chosen to help Audi's used car division increase their market share. At the time, their product was known as *Audi Assured*—a good name—but people were confused about the product. In short order, it was renamed Audi Certified Pre-Owned. Today, both Kia and Audi are leaders in this segment.

Stake Your Identity

To further illustrate the importance of naming, the brilliant engineering firm, Betts Industries, had invested years designing and perfecting a pressure relief valve that was truly superior to the competition. It, along with its competitors' products, was simply known as a "DOT 407 vent" due to being associated with a Department of Transportation (DOT) code.

A quick Google search of "407 vent" yielded pages of competitors' products claiming the ultimate solution as well. Betts was lost in that maze. Betts, whose slogan is *Do What's Best*, had designed this product for the right reason: to protect the end-user. Our team knew that story needed to be told. The most powerful way to do that was by naming it, and the "Guardian" was born. One word explained it all. Having its own identity set it apart from dozens of faceless competitors. Who would you trust to protect your life, a 407 vent or the "Guardian"?

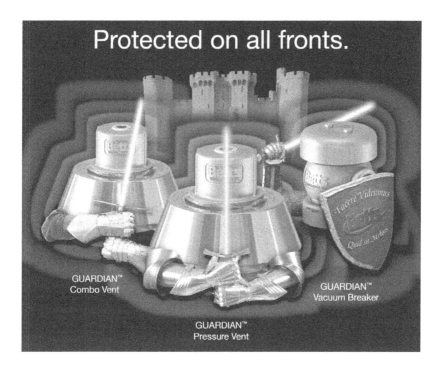

This armed their sales team to tell the story behind how and why the Guardian was engineered and designed. Betts now stood out from the pack because only they had the "Guardian" while everyone else merely had a "407 vent."

Working with advanced engineering firms like Betts Industries brings to light that companies are often too humble or understated in their product positioning. It is not bragging or bravado if you've developed an outstanding product. You owe it to your customers to inform and educate them, to help them make an informed decision about whether to buy or not. Your employees deserve to know that they represent a company that is doing the right things.

In a world where customers scour websites and conduct countless Google searches, you can't assume they'll choose or even notice your offerings unless you stand out. Be the product with that unique name and inspiring story.

Universally Powerful

In 1965, Stephen Salyer and his wife Stephanie started a company in Southern California. It primarily focused on janitorial services for businesses. Steve approached his attorney, Jack Salyer (his father's cousin), for advice on what to name their new venture. Despite it being a two-person company at the time, Steve wanted to make sure that their name was impressive. Jack suggested the name, "Universal." Steve loved how it positioned his company as substantial and formidable. Over the next few years, they added security guard services to their offerings and became known as Universal Protection Services. That small, upstart janitorial and security service steadily grew, organically and through acquisitions. Today it is known as Allied Universal and is the seventh largest employer in the world with 800,000 employees in ninety countries. Steve's success was aided by his understanding of the power of a word, *universal*.

Naming Should Clarify, Not Confuse or be Too Clever

When my wife, Carol, and I were newly married, I surprised her with her dream car, an Acura Legend (it was used but in great shape, and this was before CPO cars!). Over the next five years, she loved the Legend; it was her pride and joy. When it was time to buy a new vehicle, she announced, "I love this Legend so much, I want my next car to be an Acura. Let's go to the dealership!"

We arrived there to see some beautiful products. The problem was, we couldn't decipher which ones were which. The models all had names that were unclear: a CL, an RL, RDX, and MDX. I couldn't easily figure out what the letters meant. Which one was entry level, and which one was the luxury model?

The salesperson educated me, somewhat: "Our product line-up is hard to explain because we're not like Mercedes where you know a C-class is below the D-class and so on. But our cars are great."

She was certainly correct; their models are excellent. But why allow the naming of your product to create barriers or confusion? I firmly believe that Acura would have far greater market share if they were clearly positioned and named.

Name It and Create a Premium

Kenneth Ricci is a genius. He's an author, attorney, pilot, entrepreneur, and leader of numerous aviation companies, including Flexjet. After he acquired it, he set out to create a new, even more premium level of Flexjet offerings by upgrading its fleet and pilot teams, and personally designing the interiors of the jets himself.

What Kenn did next was just as impressive. He *named* this new, higher level of offering. Today, Flexjet *Red Label* is known as the ultimate experience in aviation, attracting the discriminating customer who values perfection and exactitude in every detail.

Meet FRED

Manufactured products are usually looked at as "things" that are then assigned numbers and sold along with, and often against, other things with numbers. A chassis manufacturer created a breakthrough product, designating it "22407." It was a best-kept secret and possessed powerful advantages, including superior handling and excellent MPG (miles per gallon), yet it sold poorly. Those who bought it loved it, though. The company's marketing team included the 22407 in their brochures and promotional materials, along with the other half dozen chassis they offered (which all were identified by numbers as well, such as the "24309"). It just didn't stand out. Then the old 22407 was given a new name, a *real name*, and brought to life.

The 22407 was transformed into "FRED," which was short for *Front Engine Diesel*. Their dealers shared its story along with why it differed from a standard chassis. It became "cool" to refer to this inanimate object as FRED. Without a single technical improvement, price reduction, or major increase in the marketing budget, FRED became a bestseller.

The chassis had been given a personality; it stood out and, unlike any other it competed against, was "fun." This gave birth to a new segment of chassis that the competition eventually had to participate in, as customers were frequently asking if they too offered a FRED.

The chassis formerly known as the 22407 had become the Kleenex of their industry. Giving your product a meaning, a name, and best of all, a personality will transform you from being an MP3 player to being an iPod—from being the 22407 to being known affectionately as FRED.

It's All in the Name

Once you name your differentiator, be consistent. Industry-leading brand THERABAND had long ago created a color-based system to help guide their customers (clinicians) to use their elastic resistance bands and products safely and effectively. No one in the industry offered anything this brilliant.

But there was a problem. Over decades, the color system lost its identity and was copied by competitors, being referred to by many names and non-names, including Progression System, Color Code or Resistance Band Color Program. It took strong leadership to end that. Kevin Turner, Vice President, Brand & Product, and David Wells, Senior Product Manager, rallied their organization to commit to a singular name for this breakthrough: The Trusted Progression™ System. No longer referred to by multiple names and now trademarked, it became easy for sales representatives to sell it and clinicians to ask for it. The Trusted Progression System became a major asset to their brand once again and clearly repositioned them as the premium product in the segment.

The Venturi Effect

Michael DiMino is a renowned CEO celebrated for his ability to revitalize companies to extraordinary heights. As the leader of TriStar Industrial in Phoenix, his exceptional performance during the company's acquisition by the respected private equity firm Trive Capital caught the attention of their leaders: Jared Reyes, Jay Vise, and Danny Valiente. Seeking to create a larger brand, Trive merged TriStar Industrial with three other PVF (pipes, valves, and fittings) firms. When it came to naming this new venture, they aimed for a distinctive and meaningful identity that transcended the generic names commonly associated with holding companies.

After an extensive process of research and collaboration, our team presented "Venturi" as the ideal name. It pays homage to Giovanni Venturi, the nineteenth-century discoverer of the Venturi effect—a phenomenon where the velocity of fluid increases while passing through a constricted section of a pipe, leading to a decrease in pressure. The name *Venturi* aligns with their core principles of efficiency and expertise, plus establishes a memorable, original brand identity.

Once you identify a unique product or system, name it, give it meaning, and honor it. Tell its story. Realize that your customers don't have the interest or energy to wade through internet searches to learn what makes you different. Make it as easy as possible. Make it fun and interesting. Name it.

CHAPTER 7

LESSONS FROM THE COURT AND THE DIAMOND

DIFFERENTIATION IS IMPORTANT IN ALL AREAS of life, not just in business. The experiences shared in this chapter enriched the lives of many, including me. And they armed me to better search for uniqueness with our clients.

At a fifth-grade girls' basketball game, the team's tallest girl jogged slowly down the court. Her father yelled out, "Lizzy, take your hands out of your pockets!" A parent sitting nearby leaned in and said to him, "You're funny—why are you yelling that at her?" Her dad turned and quickly replied, "Because that girl running down the basketball court past us is my daughter and her hands are in her pockets. It's hard to handle the ball that way!"

Lizzy's dad was a decent guy, but he was missing the point. After the game, the two of them sat down to discuss things. Lizzy confessed, "I really don't like basketball."

Her dad couldn't believe what he'd heard. "But you're five inches taller than any other girl on your team and we live in Indiana! You have to love basketball, right?"

Lizzy stood tall (which was easy for her) and said, "I want to paint and draw things. I love being creative. Can I please do that instead?"

A brand, just like the children we love, can't be all things to all people. If Lizzy's dad forced her to be something she wasn't and play basketball, she'd end up as that kid who got a full-ride scholarship and dropped out of college, miserable and broken, along with having a terrible relationship with her father. Sure, she was tall and could "shoot the rock," but that didn't mean this was where to find her passion or uniqueness. In business jargon, the situation wasn't sustainable.

Your brand is the same. Just because you can do it doesn't mean that you should. I learned—I mean, Lizzy's dad learned his lesson. Her future WNBA career was over, but now she could wake up each morning excited without feeling pressure to be someone or something she wasn't. Similarly, a company that is genuinely differentiated can wake up to face the day confidently, knowing who they are, ready to fight business battles on their own terms.

Snapping the Streak

When my daughter, Laura Elizabeth (I nicknamed her Lizzy), was young, her small elementary school approached me to coach the basketball team, which I soon learned was in the throes of a one-hundred-game losing streak. That explained why I received this "opportunity" after the previous coach, a grandparent of two of the players, walked off in understandable frustration. With this collection of fourth, fifth, and sixth grade girls, I knew I was in over my head and turned to an expert. I begged my friend, Joe Sowder, a former college basketball player, to coach with me since I was more of a cheerleader than a basketball savant like him.

I thought our first practice was going well until Joe gathered the girls and declared, "Since you won't probably ever see me again, here are some tips I have for you…" I noticed the shocked and disappointed expressions on the girls' faces and begged him to stay. He said, "I can't believe how difficult it is to get these girls to play ball." Joe was accustomed to much older, established players, and, truthfully, the girls were a little immature. The fact that only an hour earlier two of them needed to be separated during a locker room deathmatch fighting over a boy reinforced his point. This was just the first of several times Joe's resolve was tested, but, to his credit, he made it through the year, and we snapped the losing streak—all by discovering the strengths and differentiation of each player.

Joe's keen basketball sense identified one girl as a strong defender, while another was a great rebounder but reluctant shooter. The tallest girl handled the ball well and was our best shooter, but she didn't like to rebound. We had one much older player, who we were told was a bit "slow." Joe transformed her into our fiercest defender. (I often told her gently, "Nice job, but next time please be a little less violent.") None of the girls on their own could take control of the game, and the team was far from perfect, but when they each did what they did best, they could compete.

We went 5–5 that year, surprisingly good after that one-hundred-game losing streak. Not only did they perform well together, but they also loved playing and were truly a wonderful team. The next season under a different coach (another parent) they were undefeated. I was envious of his success and asked him how he did it.

He confided, "I realized that all these years our opponents were much larger schools than ours and would send their sixth grade 'varsity' team to play us. Being much smaller, we had fewer players available and had to combine our fourth, fifth, and six graders into one team, which wasn't fair. So, I asked the other schools to send their 'junior varsity' (fourth graders) only. Since then, we've dominated!"

It pays to look at the competition a lot closer than I did during my one year at the helm!

Play Ball

My son, Alan, from the time he was three years old, was a jock, hitting "flop shots" over fir trees swinging a real (cut-down) golf club. Five years later, after winning Junior Golf tournaments, he made a hole-in-one. He then "retired" from golf to become a baseball player, eventually concluding his sports career as a top D2 college starting pitcher.

I coached his baseball teams until he was beyond my level of expertise, around the time he reached thirteen or fourteen. We had some decent and some not-so-decent squads, but we always had fun. They performed at their best and loved doing it because we always focused on the strength of each player.

There was a quiet, twelve-year-old boy on one of his teams, a great fielder. I proudly told his mom at the end of practice one day, "Teddy sure can play a great third base. He has a lot of talent fielding the ball and is the fastest player on the team." His mother looked at me and laughed. She replied, "Are you talking about *my* Teddy? At home, he's slow, clumsy, and I clean up after him all the time. You must be confusing him with some other boy on the team!" It's easy to overlook what is special when you're around it every moment. Teddy had so much talent that I often joked with him after he'd make a tremendous catch in the field. "Hey, Teddy," I'd call out. "Yeah, Coach?" I'd then say dismissively, "That catch was okay" and we'd both grin at each other. It was important to have that personal connection, just as it is with your customers and employees.

One of the strengths of our teams was that every player had a nickname. This was a rule of ours, every bit as important as "bring your glove." Baseball lore is filled with great monikers: "The Mick," "The Say Hey Kid," "Shoeless" Joe Jackson, "The Babe," and so on. At each of my son's games, we'd announce the lineup over the loudspeaker, along with the players' nicknames, which were their differentiators. This made it more fun, and it shone a light on each player's individuality.

Here's an example of our lineup:

- Billy "Wild" Thane (fast but control-challenged pitcher)
- Jimmy "Little Feller" (Hall of Famer, Bob Feller's great-grandson)
- Kelson "Special K" (a great kid who made "basket catches" in the outfield, like Willie Mays did)
- Alan "The Energizer" (fastest, hardest-working kid on the team)
- Eric "Secretary of Defense" (best fielder)
- Maddie "The Human Vacuum Cleaner" (great infielder, no ball got past her)
- Justin "Big Unit" (tallest kid on the team)
- Tommy "The Toy Cannon" (diminutive but powerful hitter)
- Billy "Big Papi" (his favorite player was David "Big Papi" Ortiz)

OFFICIAL BATTING ORDER

		POS.
1	Billy "Wild" Thane	1
2	Jimmy "Little Feller"	6
3	Kelson "Special K"	8
4	Alan "The Energizer"	5
5	Eric "Secretary of Defense"	9
6	Maddie "The Human Vacuum Cleaner"	4
7	Justin "Big Unit"	3
8	Tommy "The Toy Cannon"	2
9	Billy "Big Papi"	7

I knew the parents loved that their children had been given these special identities. But when an opposing coach walked up to me scowling before a game, it proved to be clearly powerful. "Look, you have these cool names for your kids. It's not fair." Bizarre but true. He and I then sat down and created monikers for each of his players. His team's parents heard the names announced over the baseball field's PA system and cheered on.

And to take it one more step, we celebrated at the conclusion of every season, no matter our record, to recognize the strengths of the players. Each received their own trophy—not one of those crappy "participation" awards but one with their nickname and what they did that was special. This was our team's version of an internal branding celebration. All family members were invited to join in the festivities as well. It was a highlight for everyone who took part. Like the internal celebrations we urge clients to conduct, these events rallied the team to better appreciate each other.

As a result of this focus on differentiation, we also had an unintended problem: every kid wanted to come back to our team the next year (which was not allowed in Little League). Our retention was too high!

How powerful was this? One day years later, one of my employees told me a note was left on a pizza box. (Our office had ordered lunch from a local Italian restaurant and the young girl who dropped it off said, "Please give this to Mr. LaBov.") Turns out, she was the player on my daughter's basketball team, who was supposedly a "little slow," the one who was the fierce defender. It read: "Dear Coach, I scored twenty points and grabbed fifteen rebounds for my high school team Tuesday night!" She added, "I wasn't too violent, either!" And not long after, I was in a store when a woman approached me to say, "Hi, Coach, remember me? I'm Wild Thane's mom!"

Yes, you can have fun discovering, naming, and celebrating your differentiation.

CHAPTER 8

CAN YOU DELIVER YOUR EXPERIENCE?

IN THIS CHAPTER, WE DIVE INTO THE VALUE of brand experiences. A strong brand experience builds value in the minds and hearts of customers, inspiring loyalty. Here are three examples of experiences that not only fell short but were also total disconnects for customers:

A manufacturer (it produced both consumer and industrial products) positioned itself as an inspiring, technological leader. Yet, when customers visited their website, they discovered it was an ancient artifact with broken links and outdated images. To make matters worse, the products were impossible to order. Customers gave up, moved on, never to return.

A retail brand portrayed itself as fun, stylish, and hip, yet when customers made the journey to visit the stores, they found them outdated, rundown, and staffed with people you'd never imagine would buy the brand. As a result, customers walked in, observed the situation, immediately turned around and left.

An upstart industrial pump producer was awarded a huge bid because they convinced the customer they would "provide the utmost in personalized service." But soon, the customer and her team experienced the "real" brand when reaching out for help after the unit failed. Emails went unanswered, and pleas for assistance on their toll-free "help" line were put on hold for twenty minutes until a recording announced, "Please call back during regular business hours." The customer's next move was to run down to their legal department to find a way to cancel the contract.

These examples all illustrate how a brand's experience can be out of sync with what they claim.

One Company's Customer Experience Mastery

I purchased an Apple computer, loved it, but it soon developed a problem overheating and frequently shutting down. Enduring it for a while, I finally called the "VAR" (Value Added Retailer—the distributor I bought it from) and asked him to solve the issue.

He reluctantly agreed but not without first informing me, "Don't be surprised if Apple ignores my request to help you." A week later he let me know, as predicted, they would not assist him. My only option (other than to suffer through the computer going "dark" daily) was to personally call their service help line because, as he said, "Apple will respond to customers, but they don't care about VARs." This made no sense to me because I assumed Apple valued their distribution system. All this made me doubt their genius (but hang in there, I just wasn't smart enough to understand it!).

I called the customer help line and was promptly asked for my information, including if I was a customer or VAR. Hmmm, interesting. Then I spoke with a pleasant person who informed me that my computer was now two weeks out of warranty, but he'd see what he could do.

Next, I was connected with a supervisor, a woman with an outstanding personality. Her first words were: "Honey, you've had the exact same problem as other customers. We've since fixed the faulty component issue. Yes, you're out of warranty, but Apple will ship you a brand-new computer immediately. One more thing, sweetie: consider purchasing the extended warranty, just in case."

I thanked her, bought the warranty (maybe that was a sales ploy, but, hey, I'm getting a new computer!) as I fell even more deeply in love with Apple.

What I witnessed was the battle between a brand and their sales channel over who owns the customer. Apple's strategy exposed that the VAR was little more than an intermediary in their eyes. And in their case, they were right because today, my loyalty belongs to Apple, my trusted friend. I honestly don't remember the VAR's name, but I'll never forget that Apple took care of me.

I don't recommend this approach for most businesses. In fact, I believe it will prove unsuccessful for 90 percent of the companies that sell through a distribution channel, causing turmoil and severing relationships.

But this does illustrate how invaluable it is to design and control the experience your customers receive.

Questions to Identify and Improve Your Brand Experience

If you want to understand how customers or clients view your brand and seek ways to improve their experience with it, consider the following nine questions.

1. Do you have a defined, consistent experience?

Or do you have two, three, or eight hundred of them? If your sales channel has eight hundred salespeople and no defined customer treatment standards, then there are that many experiences of varying quality with absolutely no consistency. Pleasing anyone (customers, dealers, and the enterprise itself) is impossible in that predicament.

2. Is your experience authentic?

If you call yourself the "Fun Car Company" yet stick it to customers because the goal is to close deals at any cost, it's obvious that your brand is disingenuous. I pre-ordered a car from a dealer, waited nine months, finally picking it up during a winter evening blizzard. I asked the salesperson if he was confident this was the right car. It looked "blacker" than the blue I ordered, but then again, it was pitch dark outside and we were in the middle of a storm. He assured me it was correct, and I drove home.

I discovered after the snow melted the next morning that it was indeed the wrong one. I called him and asked for the model I ordered, only then learning they had already sold it a week prior. I informed him that despite their name, The Fun Car Company, it was no fun being their customer right now and I expected to be satisfied.

The salesperson received no support from his ownership, another sign that their slogan was just an empty promise. Three weeks later, I got the car I demanded from them, after they scoured dealerships nationwide to find one that fit my original order. I vowed never to buy from the dealer again. This lackluster experience was made even worse because their slogan promised the opposite. If their mantra had been "We're the cheap car company," I would have been more likely to accept this treatment.

3. Is your sales channel dedicated or "playing the field?"

To put this another way, is your product the only one in its category that your dealer sells, or do they represent others as well? If they offer only your brand, it's far more likely they'll support a consistent, refined experience. A VP of customer service at a UTV (Utility Terrain Vehicle) brand said, "Our dealers didn't think our units were special or unique, so they sold us at the lowest price point. We responded to this by training them the best we could on our products, which were nowhere close to being leaders in the segment. But the big thing we focused on was our relationship *with the dealer;* we wanted to be their best friend.

Soon, that became *the* differentiator for us. We were the rare brand that responded to them, took care of their customer issues immedi-ately, and functioned as a true partner. And the more we invested in this strategy, the more our channel and customers fell in love with our brand." It's worth noting that this UTV company benefited most from focusing on their dealer relationships, as their product was certainly, at best, viewed as the middle of the pack.

4. Do your sales channel experiences reflect the quality of treatment you want to offer customers?

We helped a European auto manufacturer relaunch their brand in the U.S. Their executives had long been frustrated with the dealer net-work's performance, especially regarding customer treatment, feeling it was less than trustworthy or inspiring.

As part of our process, we interviewed not only the brand's execu-tives but also dealer principals. Dealers told us clearly that the relation-ship with the auto brand had been challenging, and that, interestingly, a lack of trust was felt on *both* sides. We helped our client understand it was clearly unreasonable to expect dealers to treat customers with respect unless both they (the brand) and dealer modeled that same behavior with each other. From that point on, they developed a rela-tionship based on integrity. This sounds easy, but both parties had to face issues openly and solve them together, ushering in a new era as they reinvigorated their partnership. In time, this led to dealers deliv-ering premium customer treatment as they mirrored the behavior they received from the manufacturer.

5. Do you "live" the brand and associate with the customer?

A few, very amazing companies overflow with people who not only represent the brand but are also customers and ambassadors of it. Their leaders and employees love the product, experiment with it, and hang out with customers. If your company produces snowmobiles, does your team ride them as well? Or, on the opposite end of the spectrum, do you manufacture a "value" offering, yet top executives personally own a competitor's premium brand instead? If so, analyze the message being sent, because others are watching to see if you really believe.

6. Is customer loyalty rewarded?

Most of us think of airline rewards programs when it comes to customer retention, but is it really loyalty if we are "bribing" people with points and free products to stay with us? With most customers, merely being acknowledged, thanked, and confided in are enough for them to stay with you (assuming your product works, of course).

Several years after the luxury car brand Lexus was launched, they mailed current customers a survey asking for feedback on the car and suggestions for future products. Lexus explained they were in the process of designing their next iteration and valued the feedback of loyal customers. Thousands responded, excited that they had been asked to take part.

Think about it: those customers most likely had previously owned products from Mercedes-Benz, BMW, or another luxury brand, never having been asked for that level of input. It was a brilliant move, especially since, within a year, the next Lexus model was launched and was an immediate hit with the very people who *felt* they had influenced it. Not to burst a bubble, but I find it highly unlikely that survey influenced the new model, as it had been in the works for at least three years, which is common in the industry. But the Lexus customer had been treated with respect, and that was reward enough.

7. Are employees empowered to solve problems?

Your team will usually know far better how to help the customer than anyone else. The best brands promote an internal strategy encouraging people on the front line to solve problems immediately. You will dramatically improve both customer loyalty and employee retention by doing this.

When I encountered issues with my Apple computer, as I shared earlier, a supervisor greeted me on the phone and offered a solution. She must have been well-trained in her freedom as well as constraints in solving problems. Had she handed it off to another department and I had to endure more drama with the defective product, Apple would have lost a customer and risked the possibility of me complaining to others about them. Instead, her solution was well-received and my loyalty to the brand grew.

I had a similar situation with Sleep Number mattresses and after encountering great frustration, I did a "blind" reach out on LinkedIn to their CEO, in hopes of a resolution. The next day, I received a call from the CEO's administrative assistant and within short order, they took care of the issue. I'm still a loyal Sleep Number customer to this day.

8. Does your technology help or hinder the experience?

Whether it's your website, email system, app, or call lines, if they present one more arduous task to endure when a problem occurs, you're in a battle to keep customers. Technology should not be in place purely to make it easier or cheaper for you. It is primarily in place to assist the customer.

Amazon has created a technological relationship for all who visit their site. Few of us speak to a "live" Amazon employee. Instead, their online user experience is seamless and designed to remove barriers (for example, their return policy), promote trust (product reviews), and assist you by sharing what others just like you purchased. Their technology encourages customer trust.

9. How accessible is leadership?

What if there's a major customer issue or opportunity? Will the "top dog" jump in immediately? You can build lifelong relationships when the customer knows you care. If the leader is never available to discuss a situation, that makes a statement. Also, sometimes it's wonderful when a customer hears from the president.

In the early days of Tesla, an extremely wealthy businessman placed an order with one of their representatives. He was told they would review his credit report and, if approved, process it. Once the finance team saw who the individual was, they immediately took action.

Minutes later, the rep called back. "Would you hold? Mr. Musk would love to personally thank you for choosing Tesla." The businessman pondered for a moment, wondering, "Who's Mr. Musk?" and said, "No, thanks" and hung up the phone. They never did speak. The fact that Elon Musk paid attention to who bought his product shows his involvement in every aspect of his then fledgling brand. At that point, Mr. Musk was accessible. Maybe not so much now.

And as an owner of four Teslas, I can attest that their customer treatment has dramatically changed over the years, dampening my enthusiasm for the product. Originally, their service reps were very helpful and friendly, assisting in the buying process. Now, with their more automated approach, it's impersonal, and at times, infuriating. That lackluster connection with the customer can give the competition an edge, which is why I purchased a Lucid.

Amazing Customer Experience

I've encountered a few outstanding brands whose market success was astounding. My team was asked to rebrand a successful company that dominated an industry. At first, we pondered the root of their success. Maybe it was segment-leading design, or they possessed a technology no one else had. We soon learned they were strong in these areas, but there was far more to the story.

As we interviewed customers and dealers, we were immediately intrigued with what was shared. Customers described their opinion of the brand using words and terms such as "love" and "God bless them," often unheard of when discussing a manufacturer.

Dealers, likewise, spoke of how they and the company were "family" when describing their interactions. It became clear the brand's primary focus was on *relationships*—with suppliers, dealers, employees, and customers. Everyone pitched in with no boundaries.

We conducted our Technical Immersion at the plant, which was the brightest, most illuminated factory we'd seen. It was run with clock-work precision. Everything was focused on simplifying all aspects of production, which, in turn, ultimately reduced mistakes and quality issues for the dealer and customer.

As we toured their plant, we met employees who were extraor-dinarily friendly and curious about our team. They proudly told us it was common for customers to tour the facility, hang out with them, and develop lifelong friendships, even direct dialing "Carl in the paint shop" or "Dottie in purchasing" to ask questions and chat. Impressively, leadership understood the value of this, encouraging employees to connect with the special people, their customers, who traveled there to buy the brand.

Concluding our process, it had become clear this company had mastered the art *and* science of "the experience" and their suppliers, dealers, customers, and employees were beneficiaries. It was their edge against the competition, which in many cases, had strained, sterile re-lationships with customers and dealers.

Many companies make promises, sell a product to you, and that's the end of it. With this rare brand, once the customer chooses their unit, that's when the experience really begins. This loyalty to employees, suppliers, dealers, and customers was reciprocated, propelling them to lead their industry. Their experience *was* their brand differentiation.

Just as an inspired customer experience can be your calling card, a poor one may threaten to close your doors.

Sometimes great people are trapped in and can't break free from a culture. When interviewing Danny, a charming Englishman who was the customer service VP of an HVAC manufacturer, I asked about the brand's customer service. He looked down, sighed, and fessed up. "I'm embarrassed to admit it, but we avoid dealing with issues. We have a complaint line, but those calls go directly into voicemail. About ev-ery two weeks, the messages are typed up and emailed to our dealers, handing off the problems to them." Danny found this appalling. He feared the company would not survive without dramatically reversing their position that the dealer owned all customer issues.

The company's leaders were bottom-line focused and calculated, surmising that this strategy saved money. Danny shared, "Our team feels that, after all, the dealer sold the product, why can't they handle the crap?" While logical, we both agreed that the customer doesn't distinguish the dealer from the brand. If the product is not working, it hurts everyone involved. That applies to cars, jets, as well as heating and air conditioning systems.

Danny then revealed his company's recent customer survey results, which were as he said, "in the tank." It was no surprise, as they had allowed hundreds of unhappy consumers to wait weeks for a response from their local dealers, who understandably, were also embarrassed and furious, as well.

Danny corrected this nightmare, replacing their voicemail customer service line with a well-trained team of impassioned employees ready to answer all inquiries immediately. In short order, they learned that customers and dealers were usually very reasonable when dealt with promptly and respectfully. However, Danny was right: years of neglect had its consequences. Hundreds of customers left the brand, never to return. Their top dealers "jumped ship" to represent competitors. Danny persevered until he could escape from there as the company floundered, underperforming until it was sold.

Sweet Success

Chuck Surack founded Sweetwater Music, which, from humble beginnings, became the world's largest online music retailer. Chuck and I have been friends for decades since he recorded my rock band in his garage studio, playing saxophone on our songs. His company's success is due in part to the customer experience he and his team developed.

At Sweetwater, there are no salespeople, there are *sales engineers*. A sales engineer interacts via phone with musicians from all over the world and helps them determine which product to purchase. These musicians know their stuff, so Sweetwater makes sure whoever represents their thousands of products has passion for and expertise in music equipment. It all comes down to education and preparation.

Each new sales engineer undergoes extensive product and industry training for thirteen weeks before they are slowly eased into customer contact, as they spend most of their days being educated in over one hundred different subjects ranging from product information to the history of rock music.

This substantial investment in each person reaps benefits as they grow to be experts, master the customer base, and embody their distinctive culture. This has armed Sweetwater to win the battle against brick-and-mortar music stores as well as online companies. In a world of impersonal, virtual interactions, Chuck devised a customer experience that sets them apart from everyone else.

It's interesting to note that while Sweetwater sells technological products, their customer experience is, in many ways, non-technological. It would have been simpler for them to imitate Amazon by selling primarily through their website. Instead, Chuck took a personalized, differentiated approach, giving his company a distinct advantage. At Sweetwater, while you may purchase the exact same guitar, microphone, or keyboard you'd find elsewhere, your "sales engineer" is your trusted friend and guide, and that experience makes a difference.

From Taking Orders to Orchestrating Possibilities

The words you use as a leader can derail a brilliant vision for your brand. A wealth management firm hired a dynamic yet polarizing marketing executive to upgrade their customer experience. He quickly assessed the situation and, in a booming voice, announced to their client service team that they were "order-takers." You can imagine how that made them feel.

Approaching me he said, "I need you to fix these people. They're good, smart, and all that, but they bring too little value to our clients. We're losing market share because of them."

Their client service did have room for improvement. But how could he expect people to change when they already thought they were doing an excellent job? Knowing that this proud team would not receive anything a stranger (my firm) would suggest to them, I turned to the one source they cared about: their clients.

The clientele loved their service representatives but told us they'd like even more input and guidance from them. This was a systemic issue in the firm. In their over one hundred years of serving the nation's wealthiest families, they had become a sleeping giant, primarily focused on protecting their business, which meant trying not to irritate or bother their clients. The easiest way, they felt, to maintain that relationship was to say "yes" and avoid making waves. But, we also learned in some cases their top reps performed amazingly. Clients raved about those rare occasions. Our goal, then, became to shine a spotlight on those performances to encourage even more of them.

One client boasted that his rep saved him $10k a month on insuring his exotic car collection. That's almost unfathomable, but it made the point: resourcefulness and guidance were deeply valued. This heroic testimonial and others were captured on video, as clients shared stories of their rep's expertise and how it made a difference. This opened the hearts and minds of the team, having far more impact than an executive criticizing them for being order-takers.

Our team then conducted "Best Day" workshops (more about them below), engaging the team to discover how they worked together in their absolute best moments to create these tremendous outcomes. These fantastic performers had passion and expertise. All they needed was to slightly alter their perception of what the client desired and how they could please them. It was purely positive and inspiring. It provided them with an even deeper understanding of their roles.

Unfortunately for the marketing executive, he was soon ushered out the door, proving that while you may be right, your words and actions can betray you.

Best Day

We conduct workshops after a client discovers their differentiation to help them refine their brand experience. Participants will first work together in teams to identify their *best days*: those times when everything seems to flow, where people help each other, and clients love collaborating with them.

We then pose a simple question: "How often do you have that kind of day?" Answers range from ten times a year to "almost never." The goal is to create more "best days."

For the remainder of the workshop, participants explore how they can improve their internal and external experience. The customer will certainly benefit from this, but, just as important, employees will as well, resulting in greater fulfillment and satisfaction in their job.

Are Our Best Days Behind Us or In Front of Us?

Don Hunter, Chief Operating Officer of Country Club of North Carolina (CCNC) in Pinehurst, North Carolina, is a dear friend and an inspiration. He has led country clubs and golf clubs, including CCNC, Quail Creek CC (Naples, Florida), Chapel Hill CC (Chapel Hill, North Carolina), and Sycamore Hills Golf Club in Fort Wayne, Indiana. Don is a tireless leader who has amazed me with his energy and positivity. A key to his success is in asking his staff one simple question when he joins them, "Are our best days behind us or are they ahead of us?" Don will usually learn what is in the way of progress for the very people who are entrusted to provide the member experience at their clubs. Interestingly, it's not as easy as it sounds. Don shared, "Often, I'll hear that some barrier is in the way. It's my job to remove it and give the team the chance to do what they've been dreaming of. And those barriers can be challenging, depending on the situation. In my experience, people can do remarkable things on their best days; my job is to give them more of those days."

Your Experience Affects Employees, Customers, and Leaders

Shortly before the 2008 recession crushed our economy, I was approached to attend a secret meeting at my golf club, Sycamore Hills Golf Club (Fort Wayne, Indiana). I was one of the younger guys in the boardroom as two older, wiser, local statesmen shared that the club could be sold (or possibly out of business) at any moment, due to the founder being in failing health. A number of highly successful people were at the table that day, and I was curious who was going to lead the charge to save the club (I took note that none of them seemed very interested). It reminded me of an old cartoon I watched as a child: *Hundreds of foreign legion soldiers lined up as the general stood in front of them. He then asked which soldier was willing to volunteer for an extremely life-threatening and dangerous mission. With that, in perfect synchronization, all but one of them took a step backward. The one remaining soldier was deemed the volunteer, congratulated, and sent off to meet his fate.* As one of the statesmen concluded our meeting, he firmly announced that I was to be sent off to battle to save the club. Joining me that day was an extraordinarily successful insurance executive who grew to become one of my best friends, Morrie Sanderson. Without Morrie, we would have fallen short.

Morrie then enlisted Keith Busse, co-founder of Steel Dynamics, to help us raise money to save the club. Keith was fantastic in persuading his contacts to join us. Morrie, a brilliant negotiator, rallied investors to believe in our vision. We succeeded in buying the club, just before a competitive offer was made. It was elating. Then reality set in. In our haste to save the club, we had not been able to conduct the due diligence that would usually have been expected. The club was a gem in many ways, a Jack Nicklaus Signature course that had been a top-rated design. But we found that over the years in the haste to grow memberships, diverse deals were made, as some members didn't pay at all, others paid half the rate, while others, like me, paid full. This was news to me, but it wasn't for most of the membership. And not surprisingly, it had caused tension and turnover at the club because certain people had privileges while others didn't.

After taking charge of the club, Keith, Morrie, our General Manager, the forementioned Don Hunter, and I pledged to the entire membership that there would be no more special deals and that every-one would pay the established dues. That was received with rousing applause, ushering in a new era as all members knew they were being treated equally.

It also affected employees as they realized that they represented a club that believed in its value. How could the staff be expected to provide a world-class experience if their leaders were discounting the service? This also improved the quality of the new members, who treated the club and staff with great respect.

It takes people like Morrie and Keith who are willing to invest their reputations and energy into saving something they believe in, knowing that there would be no guarantee of return whatsoever. And it took even more courage to treat the staff and members with the respect they deserved by facing the inequity in membership dues. Seven years after we and over a dozen friends and members invested in Sycamore Hills, three of our fellow owners approached us to buy the club, resulting in each investor receiving a nice premium for their belief in the club. The new ownership then took the club to even greater heights and I'm proud to be a member to this day.

The decisions made by our team to protect the club's value by insisting on fair, consistent pricing positively influenced employees and the member experience. I benefited as well, as I invested seven years as president and while not receiving financial compensation, was richer for the friendships developed and satisfaction of knowing something as precious as Sycamore Hills Golf Club will be preserved for years to come.

Excellent brands and their leaders embrace the beauty and the value of a consistent, authentic customer experience. The entire enterprise, including employees, sales channel, and suppliers, must "live it" and embody it daily.

A positive, powerful experience gives you one more chance to overcome any issues that might arise at some point.

CHAPTER 9

RE-ENGINEER YOUR BRAND

IN THIS CHAPTER, I SHARE an overview of one of my company's key differentiators, *Brand Re-Engineering*, plus one brilliant example of how it helped a successful company become formidable. We've applied Brand Re-Engineering to over one hundred companies over the last two decades. The five-step process includes not only customer and competitive research but also deeply explores the uniqueness of a company's products, services, processes, and experience. Armed with that learning, we create messaging and deliverables that will showcase and promote your differentiation. And then, we celebrate and launch it to the most important audience first—your employees—before sharing it with the world (including suppliers, sales network, customers, and industry). Quite simply, no other approach is like it.

Most traditional branding exercises focus on the voice of the customer (VOC) interviews, move directly into creating a tagline, logo, and execution, including website, social media, and videos. The problem with this is that you miss so much valuable input. Yes, you hear what customers say, but what about the insights from employees, leadership, dealers, or the distribution network? What about the product or service itself? How is it unique? These and other key learning points are missed. That's why we created Brand Re-Engineering™.

A brand needs to be discovered, not created. It requires time and effort to allow its beauty and uniqueness to reveal itself. In my experience, it takes diligent research, scores of in-person interviews, and days of technical exploration before the story begins emerging, but after that the pieces come together beautifully.

I've been asked why we named our process Brand Re-Engineering. As Michelangelo said, *"Every block of stone has a statue inside it, and it is the task of the sculptor to discover it. I saw the angel in the marble and carved until I set him free."*

In our decades of working with great companies, most of them presented us with a brand of immense potential. Our role was to identify the beauty and power in it as we re-engineered and refined its ultimate positioning.

These are questions we often ask clients to determine if Brand Re-Engineering is a good fit for them:

- Are you an established, respected company under new leadership and looking to revitalize your brand?

- Do you fear your brand's uniqueness and value have become "lost?"

- Are you or your employees asking, "Who are we going to be when we grow up?"

- Are you introducing a new product within a year and can't afford the launch to fall short?

- Does your company have "hidden" innovations—brilliant technology, engineering, manufacturing, or service processes—that are not fully leveraged?

- Do you sell and service through a dealer, distributor, or rep network and believe they could be far more engaged?

- Are you a respected company with high-quality products, yet competitors are challenging your position?

⚡ Are your constituents (employees, sales channel, and customers) craving a more energized vision for your company's future?

Discovering Your Uniqueness and Amplifying It

Our process includes steps that no other company does. And it is a purely positive, inspiring experience for our clients and my team. We have a deep passion to help our clients (and their brands) look like heroes. That's part of our culture. We're the people behind the great people, identifying the good, the impressive, and the unique. I'll go into more depth in the following chapters, but here is an overview of our process:

Brand Assessment Research

We conduct interviews with leadership, employees, distribution, suppliers, and customers, then research the competition and audit our client's current sales, marketing, and training communication.

Our interviews are unique, both qualitative and quantitative. It takes far more time and effort to ask open-ended questions and deal with a wide range of responses, but this is necessary if you really want to learn and identify some brilliant nuggets.

Technical Immersion

At LABOV, we believe: *Your brand lives inside your products and processes.* In this step, we dive into your processes, products, features, and technologies to discover what makes you unique. There is power behind your procedures, metallurgy, components, materials, machinery, and technology. There are fascinating reasons your engineers reinforce a vehicle's walls in a particular fashion or why they applied their genius to reduce the number of chassis welds to improve product integrity. If it exists, we will find it.

To some, this may seem excessive and unnecessary, but it's the opposite as this exploration routinely allows us to produce break-throughs for our clients. My team has perfected the art and science of the Technical Immersion and loves seeing our clients' eyes light up knowing their brilliant products or processes are now an integral part of the brand's story.

Brand Strategy Roadmap

After we have learned from the people behind the brand and delved into the product and processes themselves, we ensure our recommendations support the company's vision of the future. We ask clients to share their five-year strategic plan, including market share goals, metrics, and new product development. For example, if the company plans to eliminate a particular product or market segment, it's best to identify that as soon as possible to reduce wasted effort.

Armed with that vision, we conduct "jam sessions," inviting clients to join us to help produce their Brand Strategy Roadmap. In these meetings, we share insights and recommendations, including any potential disconnects that need to be addressed. Here, we will recommend the product features and processes considered "differentiators" as well. Before we adjourn, we will have created a step-by-step plan to roll out the brand.

This Roadmap is then shared with the entire leadership team in a spirited conversation that will energize and spark powerful breakthroughs and deep commitment. All this exciting learning and inspiration takes place *before* execution of a logo, tagline, or video.

Brand Execution and Deliverables

At this point, clients are free to take our Brand Strategy Roadmap "in house" if they prefer their internal team tackle the execution. More often, they ask us to continue partnering with them on creation of the logo, tagline, lexicon, and brand guidelines that serve as a "North Star" for future messaging. We apply all learning and strategy accomplished in our first three steps to create a wide range of deliverables ranging from social media, websites, and technologies to marketing and training content, all with a singular, inspiring vision. And then it's time to launch!

Internal Launch and (Ultimately) External Launch

Our fifth and final step is powerful: launching and celebrating the new branding and differentiation to the most important audience *first*: your employees. This is exciting and rewarding. They hear it and feel it from you before the dealer, industry, or customer does. You acknowledge them for their contributions as they played an important role in the process and embody the brand itself.

We recommend making this a special event. Halt all production in the plant or the offices. Stop the world for a few minutes. We've seen clients orchestrate this in thirty-minute "huddles" as well as half-day celebrations.

Following this, consider a similar rollout to your distribution network, dealers, suppliers, or anyone who represents your brand. Then cascade it to your customers; they are part of the family and contributed as well. The launch to the media, industry, and prospects will then proceed with extraordinary support and consistency from your team.

Now, the story of a successful enterprise is made even greater.

Resurrect Your Brand and Make History

Jonathan Randall was a newly installed executive at a respected chassis manufacturer, a formerly entrepreneurial business that had become, in his opinion, slow, plodding, and corporate. "JR" was driven to change all that, pledging to revitalize the brand, declaring, "I want to make history."

His task was even more daunting because of the prior success of the business. Their competition was formidable but limited to only three players, and his company led in several of the segments. So why go through all this to *make history*? He made that clear. "We've forgotten who is in charge: the customer. We need to upend the entire culture. Today, our focus is on what's easy for us, and that must end, now."

To undertake this massive culture change meant that his team had to be receptive and supportive, which sounds easy, but when you're already successful at selling chassis and the parent company isn't complaining, it takes guts to shake things up.

It was a rival brand that spurred him to do this. That competitor had brilliantly positioned themselves as the ultimate premium product and experience, effectively cutting JR's brand out of that highly prestigious and profitable market. He couldn't stand to see this happen.

As we conducted a Technical Immersion at their plant, we discovered his brand's product had equal, if not superior, features and performance compared to this supposedly exceptional competitor. It became clear that while JR's product was at a premium quality level, it was their customer experience that fell far short. Their opportunistic competitor was capitalizing on that.

With JR's support, we created a mantra that would resonate throughout the company, positively affecting dealers and customers alike. *Driven by You* was the rally cry. It signaled that this brand was now focused on what was most important, the customer. Immediately, any product or service issue brought to the team would be solved to their satisfaction, with no delays or compromises. While inspiring as well as smart, it was also a departure and uncomfortable for the enterprise. It had to be communicated, celebrated, and trained on, over and over, until it became second nature to the employees.

JR led a celebration to inaugurate this historic moment with the entire team as customer experience training was instantly deployed throughout the company. To help cascade the movement, a "care package" was shipped to all dealers to inspire them, establishing a new standard and relationship with them. It included posters, brochures, and a personal video from leadership detailing how the brand was aligned to serve customers and be a true partner to dealers in that effort.

My memory overflows from this experience. I remember the initial meeting with JR and his confidence (some might have called it bravado) in believing that this successful, profitable brand needed to dramatically up its game. I recall huddling with proud, loyal engineers who were frustrated that their outstanding product was being viewed as second rate while knowing it was equal, if not superior to the segment-leading, premium competitor. And I still recall the smiles and assurance emanating from plant employees as *Driven by You* energized them. It was a career-defining moment for many, including me, as JR did make history.

Now, here's what's even more amazing. It sounds unbelievable, but their market share rose from 40 percent to 70 percent for most products they built. And in that coveted premium, high-end segment their competitor had dominated in, JR and team took the lead as well. And always up to tackling new challenges, Jonathan Randall is now President of Mack Trucks, North America.

The success of Brand Re-Engineering depends on the willingness of executives to be vulnerable and hungry for insights. It is also, often, the highlight of a leader's career. Next, let's take a deeper exploration of each step.

CHAPTER 10

STEP 1: BRAND ASSESSMENT

A BRAND IS TO BE DISCOVERED, not created or "forced." It's a living collection of people, products, and services that make up who you are. You can't just wake up one day and say, "I want my company's identity to be X" and expect to succeed.

The goal of Brand Re-Engineering is to discover your identity, its powerful uniqueness, and celebrate it with the world. When this happens, life gets easier. You can be who you are without the pressure to be something that you can't deliver on consistently.

The initial phase is the Brand Assessment. This is where the human aspect plays a huge role. Our goal is to listen, review all messaging, and analyze the competition. I'm privileged to have the LABOV assessment team in charge of these assignments, because of their passion to learn and help the client. Tamzen Meyer, Senior Writer, is a godsend in her research, uncovering the nuances that would usually be overlooked by me and others. Harrison Swift, VP Account Planner, Partner, at our firm, brings his deep analytical business mind to these assignments, often going toe to toe with clients on their performance metrics. Marcus McMillen, VP Creative Director, Partner, unleashes his people skills, inspiring them to unlock their true feelings toward a brand. Our clients are fortunate to have these fantastic people working on their accounts.

Like investigative reporters trying to patch together comments and input from various sources to unlock a mystery, we look for disconnects, surprises, and potential breakthroughs. It goes beyond the standard "correct" responses and instead we listen for what is "missing," as well as being on the lookout for any unique words or terms shared by interviewees. Confidentiality is ensured, so employees, customers, suppliers, and dealers are put at ease, allowing for open dialogue and greater understanding.

We use several sources of information in our search.

Voice of Customer (VOC)

Using both quantitative and qualitative research, customers are invited to share their views of the brand and why they continue to purchase its products. Often, our clients' leadership teams have conflicting opinions as to their customers and how they describe their products, the technology, the service, the relationship, or pricing. Hearing it from the customer directly helps clarify all of that and more.

Of particular attention is anything shared in the interviews that is surprising or unexpected. The usual customer-speak of "I choose them because of price or value" is not usually helpful. It's important to listen *between the lines*, noting any areas where the customer shows emotion or ramps up the energy. That's where we find the magic. We found that magic when working with entrepreneur and highly respected business leader Gary Riley. The company he had been chosen to lead had seven locations across the globe. Their customer interviews revealed widely differing opinions of the brand, all based on which location they worked with. Going forward, Gary led the charge to be "one company with one vision," which not only revolutionized their customer experience but unified their employees as well.

Courageous clients have even asked us to interview their former customers as well. This can reveal even greater insights and sometimes result in winning back the business.

Voice of Dealer, Distributor, or Channel (VOD)

The dealer (or distributor) is a unique character. Each plays the roles of customer, partner, and industry expert. Often, there is a complex relationship between them and the brand. Our interviews will reveal just how deep their commitment is and why. It's not simple, either. In some cases, dealers have no choice but to represent a brand (the competitor brands are taken) while others may sell the competition, as well. In either case, their input is valuable.

We often ask dealers what they would do if they were "in charge" of the brand they represent. They're business leaders who have strong opinions and usually share some very surprising and insightful responses. And, to make it even more fascinating, dealers are independent operators and do not all think alike. Many don't get along with each other, so let the fun begin!

Voice of Leadership or Executive (VOL)

Leaders are all unique individuals. It's critical to discover what they believe is at the heart of the brand as well as their confidence in its future. They can also be confounding, some showing little belief, others in lockstep with the president, and occasionally, we'll hear some rogue opinions. But somewhere within all of that is the answer or answers.

Messaging Audit

We inspect all marketing, communication, and training content previously and currently produced. Companies will often generate conflicting messaging over the years, including numerous slogans as well as logos with varying fonts and colors. Funny, but true, while performing a messaging audit for a worldwide manufacturing powerhouse, we discovered their marketing team had a history of dabbling with the company's logo over the years, experimenting with its colors and fonts. We recommended that they commit to one specific color formula to build consistency. The CEO spoke up in support. "I love this; now we won't have any more boardroom fights over what shade of yellow we use."

Reviewing all media, including social, collateral, and digital messaging, will also answer questions including: Does it boast of any differentiation? Is the brand clearly positioned? Are there confusing messages? Do promotional materials (print brochures, for example) need rethinking or to be eliminated? All of this will inform us as the discovery unfolds.

Voice of Supplier, Community, and Industry (VOS)

The company's choice of suppliers is a conscious decision that dramatically affects the end product and customer experience. Learning from them is critical, as they're experts in the industry, knowledgeable in the competition, and most likely to have strong opinions on your brand and operations.

Industry leaders also understand the competition and customers, and have their own independent perspective, including a historical insight of the brand. Likewise, community leaders will provide input on your organization's standing and contribution locally. All can contribute to help us unlock your identity.

Voice of Employee (VOE) Surveys

Some clients are reluctant to invite everyone on their team to take part in this process. However, we strongly recommend they do it as an opportunity to boost morale. This VOE survey is not about job satisfaction, rather it focuses on what they are most proud of and what makes the company different. Too few organizations ever ask their people for insights. This is a positive reflection of the value you see in them.

Parkview Regional Health invited its staff (thousands of doctors, nurses, and administrative professionals) to share their views on the organization and how it made an impact on the community. Responses were heartfelt and inspiring as their passion to serve patients uncovered powerful differentiation for the brand.

Competitive Research

It's fascinating, sometimes puzzling, and always insightful to learn what competitors are doing and, most of all, claiming. Where do they each position themselves? Are they similar to each other? Who is the undisputed leader and why? All this helps us to create a "lane" for your brand.

We were called in for "emergency advertising assistance" by a company that had recently re-branded itself, unknowingly copying their top competitor's identity. As they were about to launch their new advertising campaign, it was shared in advance with their top dealer who cried foul. Fortunately, that dealer also represented the competitor.

The client asked us to rescue them from the embarrassment. We initiated the Brand Re-Engineering process, listening and learning from their dealers, customers, and employees. Our Technical Immersion team uncovered differentiators that none of the competition could claim. The new branding, when completed, was unique and genuine. It also turned out to be the envy of that top competitor.

Your Brand Assessment is an enlightening endeavor that is not the answer, but it will *lead to it.* You can't effectively make changes and strides to who you want to be until you look in the mirror and appreciate who you are now.

It takes not only learning from the people behind the brand but also exploring the product, services, technology, and processes to search for true differentiation, which is what we will discuss next.

CHAPTER 11

STEP 2:
TECHNICAL IMMERSION

YOUR BRAND LIVES INSIDE YOUR PRODUCT (and your service).
There are reasons you manufacture a product a certain way, conduct
quality control checkpoints in a particular fashion, or perform specific
steps in your interactions with customers. All this and more are discovered in the second stage of the Brand Re-Engineering process, the
Technical Immersion.

To my knowledge, no other firm offers anything like a Technical
Immersion. The standard advertising and marketing agency is not
"wired" to tour a factory, being deluged with technical input, machinery, equipment, and processes, only to then distill all that into inspiring
differentiation. This is special, and it will be a highlight for your team.

The Technical Immersion includes us visiting a brand's facilities to
observe, listen, and learn. We require the brand's engineering, manufacturing, and technology leaders to describe and demonstrate every
facet of their process. This is important because we've found that after
years or decades of continually producing products and offering services, companies no longer "see" the value or brilliance in what they
are doing. A Technical Immersion helps them do that.

*A manufacturing plant may be a mile long, filled with tons of steel,
outfitted with amazing technology, and staffed with highly trained people*

who follow strict protocols. Surely, unique processes, engineering, and products are within. Here are a few brief examples of differentiation uncovered during a Technical Immersion:

Betts Industries is an exceptional engineering company that redesigned their plant's machinery for different purposes than originally intended, enabling them to ingeniously produce components at exacting quality levels their competition could not attain. This became part of their engineering story.

A leading recreational vehicle brand manufactures automotive-style, formed-aluminum (instead of wood) frames for the walls of their units, which results in a far more robust product for their customer. No competitor did that, so why not promote it?

An ambulance manufacturer inserts sound-deadening foam throughout the walls of their vehicles to reduce the decibels of noise in the cabin. This quiets the interior, allowing paramedics to better attend to patients, undistracted by traffic and road disturbances, a great testament to the brand's focus on safety.

I've encountered leaders with diverse expertise including engineering, manufacturing, accounting, sales, psychology, and even theology. My goal is to help each of them (and their teams) to view their operation with fresh eyes.

Engineers will often experience tunnel vision, dismissing a brilliant process they've devised because it's "just the right thing to do." Accountants, likewise, may scoff at the crazy investment or expensive materials needed to produce a product but not appreciate why they chose certain machinery or suppliers that provide higher quality. A marketer may neglect to acknowledge the exact lengths their team goes to in serving the customer.

All this is to be expected, but, as the Immersion progresses, clients will begin to appreciate and celebrate what makes them unique. If you don't truly value and communicate that, why should your customers or employees care?

If it costs you more or takes more time, you may have a differentiator.

Latch

A vice president of engineering in the aerospace sector described his company's recent product, which featured a life-saving innovation. "It cost us millions to develop, with all-new design and metallurgy. It's a safety latch that activates in case of emergency, due to high pressurization." When asked why they created the latch, he replied, "Well, it'll save lives." I was curious if the competition had a similar feature. He replied, "No, they don't. And we don't charge extra for it or advertise it because we don't want to come off like we're bragging." I asked, "What did you name this brilliant game-changing innovation? After pausing a moment, he smiled and answered. "We just call it 'latch.'" They expended extraordinary effort and resources into a product that saves lives; that story needed to be told. This smart company soon realized the value of its engineering and began promoting it proudly.

Grain

A food manufacturer was in search of its differentiators. We conducted a virtual Technical Immersion to discover what made them unique. The VP of manufacturing stated, "We do nothing out of the ordinary, period." The procurement VP spoke up. "I agree, we do nothing and offer nothing that is special." Wow, I could feel the excitement in the room! But then a different question was posed.

Is there any ingredient you pay more for than your competition does? Silence filled the room until the procurement VP spoke up. "We pay a significant amount extra for a special grain that we feel makes our product taste better. No other competitor has it." Suddenly, the team's energy ramped up as they shared their insights on where the grain came from, why it was superior, and how they wished their customers understood how special it was. This discovery led to promoting that ingredient and sharing its uniqueness with their employees and customer base.

A fertile place to start your search for distinctiveness is any area where you go to great lengths or pay more than the minimum to produce your product.

The Sentient Experience

Here's how we assisted a luxury service brand find their distinctiveness.

Sentient Jet Card was searching to elevate its positioning in the market. CEO Andrew Collins knew their differentiation wasn't in their jets or pilots, since their competitors could claim they offered basically the same. During our Technical Immersion, Andrew and team revealed a brilliant process they created to deliver a seamless customer experience. To their credit, they had painstakingly refined the experience over the years to the point of near perfection, and it needed to be celebrated and promoted.

For example, most of their customers didn't realize Sentient employed a back-up command center in the event of power outages or natural disasters. Nor did they understand the extensive training the pilots had to achieve or the exacting safety inspections and certifications each jet and crew had to pass to qualify to fly for Sentient. All this made their offering special. It was time to give it an identity and communicate.

They named the process *The Sentient Experience*, promoting it via white papers, social media, and websites. Customer reps were trained to share the "elevator pitch" of this industry-leading experience that provided customers peace of mind and confidence. This told the story of a brand that went to great lengths to serve the customer, positioning them as the segment leader as well as a tremendous value.

Keep in mind that the beauty of identifying your differentiation is that your major investment has already been made, whether it is in machinery, materials, technology, or service. Sentient had invested extensively in pilot certification, technology, and their command center. It was time for them to share that story and reap their deserved rewards.

Technical Immersion

A Technical Immersion is an exciting, all-hands-on-deck exploration with the very people who know and live a brand's processes, products, and technology. It's a fun, meaningful experience for all as you focus your attention on what makes you special.

We share several tips to better prepare engineering, service, technology, and manufacturing leaders to maximize their Immersion.

Explain All Processes and Conduct a No-Holds-Barred Facility Tour

Assume nothing is off limits, unimportant, or too boring to discuss. Delve into details, share stories, and don't worry about being efficient. Take the time needed to truly explain what may be unique.

Make Note of the Facility's Condition

It's critical for you to see the plant through fresh eyes, since usually numerous flaws and defects are found. Signage may need to be upgraded to better illustrate your uniqueness or processes to visitors as well as employees. Take note.

As we toured a truck body plant, we were impressed with their spotless, efficient operation. What stood out even more was that they placed signage on their machinery displaying the cost of the equipment itself—a brilliant move because it clearly illustrated their investment in the facility to employees, and customers. A strong statement is made when you see a one-million-dollar piece of equipment in front of you. It lets you know that the company is serious about what it does.

Share Stories Behind New Machinery or Technology

Why was it purchased? What does it do differently or better? What is the advantage to you (profit or efficiency, for example) and how does it benefit the end-user? You made the investment—leverage it.

Convey Additional Steps or Processes

For example, if you utilize the same sound-deadening foam *between* wall frames as your competition does, it's no big deal. But if you also apply it inside the walls themselves, share that!

Our Technical Immersion team uncovered that a manufacturer designed a specially shaped window for their units that eliminated water leaks. No competitor could boast of this. This brilliant innovation saved hassles for the customer and dealer, reducing warranty claims—that's worth telling the world!

Go Back to Your Roots

Who founded the company? Why was it created? What was the initial passion that sparked the brand? Quite possibly, it was based on an innovative product or a courageous concept that still guides the company. In 1993, Keith Busse, Richard Teets, and Mark Millett founded Steel Dynamics. These bold leaders had an inspiration: to create an extraordinary steel company where every employee, from the plant to headquarters, was rewarded for performance. That all-for-one approach lives on today and is woven throughout their brand's fabric, enabling them to compete worldwide due to their highly involved workforce and massive investments in advanced technology.

Don't Just Give Us the "Sales" Tour

Sharing the details you normally think may bore your visitors may just spur on some great discoveries. Prepare yourself for intense discussions and probing questions. No answer can be too deep or too specific.

We conducted a Technical Immersion for a manufacturer that decided their sales leader, not their engineering VP, was the best person to lead it. Despite being an outstanding sales professional, this delegation was a mistake. His answers included phrases such as these: *Well, I think we're the best, but that's my opinion. We do it this way because that's our way. We're the safest in the industry but can't claim it in our marketing because we don't have proof. There's a secret room where we experiment with new products, but you can't go in there.* Shortly after, our team had to re-conduct the Immersion with their engineering VP to truly discern their differentiation.

Think Like an Accountant and List Major Investments in the Facility

These often reveal more than dollar figures. They point to the company's passion and focus.

The forementioned Steel Dynamics invested over three billion dollars in their Sinton, Texas, facility, including hundreds of millions in machinery that delivers steel products no one else in the nation can offer.

In working with a truck manufacturer, we learned they offered a two-year guarantee on their product, as did all their competitors. But they were the only brand offering a lifetime warranty on their frame. Up to that point, that story had not been communicated to the customer. We immediately gave the warranty its own name and began promoting it.

Share Comments from Customers and Dealers about Product and Plant

Customers and dealers have a great knowledge base, as they often have experience with your competition as well. Often those insights lead to identifying key differentiators.

Review and Update Customer and Dealer Presentations

Before the Immersion, pore through your presentations to ensure all important details are shared with our team. If it's critical to a customer or dealer, we need to know. And, just as important, do those presentations need to be updated?

A manufacturer's sales leader shared his company presentation with us prior to Immersion. The PowerPoint was five years old and didn't acknowledge recent products or upgrades to the facility. It was a "downer" for that technology-based brand. They soon revised it by including innovations and differentiators discovered in their Immersion.

Share All of Your Experiments

Does your company have a passion to innovate? We've worked with brands that are relentless in their search to create something better. Tell that story, including the examples of where you fell short. The adage about Thomas Edison experimenting a thousand times until the light bulb was created may apply to you. We've worked with brands that were explorers. If that's in your DNA, it must be part of your story.

Look at Your Team

What is unique? Are they highly educated, experienced, or young? Do they come from prestigious schools or have fascinating backgrounds? Do they have interesting specialties? Do they collaborate or work alone? Do they visit with customers or dealers?

Sentient Jet is a leading jet card provider. One key member of their team is the Chief Safety Officer, who presides over the Safety Advisory Board. What provides more confidence than knowing an expert oversees the safety of every Sentient flight?

Embrace, Celebrate, and Explore

While conducting an Immersion, a manufacturer's marketing leader complained, "Our sales team still uses a fax machine for customer ordering. We actually still have green screen computers." We asked, "So, the entire company is way behind in technology?" Her response revealed what the company was all about. "No, not at all. The engineering department has the latest software and just dropped untold bucks on some new robotics, too." Going forward, their engineering processes and features were center stage in their brand messaging, and yes, they updated their sales technology as well!

Your Technical Immersion is an amazing experience. It shines a light on what makes your brand special. Once it's completed, potential differentiators will have been identified, whether they are processes, features, services, technologies, warranties, or other unique attributes. It's critical to keep in mind that, yes, differentiators will help you improve market share, but, just as important, they will inspire your employees to see and feel even more meaning and value in your brand.

Next in the Brand Re-Engineering process is the Brand Strategy Roadmap.

CHAPTER 12

STEP 3:
BRAND STRATEGY ROADMAP

UP TO THIS POINT in the Brand Re-Engineering process, our clients have opened their hearts, minds, and operations in search of uniqueness. This requires a vulnerability that should be applauded!

The next step in the journey is producing your Brand Strategy Roadmap, a document with a wealth of guidance to help the brand move forward.

Brand Passion Funnel

Our plan is organized into five phases: awareness, value, action, experience, and loyalty. It outlines how to best use PR, web presence, social media, customer experience, or training efforts to propel the brand.

Differentiators

The Technical Immersion will have revealed many differentiators. We'll focus on the top ten candidates, with the goal to land on three to five that will be named and promoted. The unique features or processes that "don't make the cut" will still be part of your story and included in messaging.

Ten Strategic Learnings

At this point, we will have uncovered numerous data points and insights. We'll highlight the ten major, highest-impact findings most critical to the enterprise. These might include recommendations to reposition a product, establish an army of brand ambassadors, refine your customer experience, or promote a specific differentiator to the world.

Brand Model

This details a brand's tangible and intangible qualities, as well as its essence. Constructed from the feedback, recommendations, and, best of all, the specific words and terms gleaned from hundreds of hours of interviews and technical exploration, this model reveals who you are and why. It is the enterprise's inspirational "North Star" and is the basis of the brand lexicon (language) as it becomes refined and focused.

Brand Strategy Roadmap Jam Session

The initial draft of the roadmap is shared with the brand's leaders and then together, we collaborate to refine and validate it further. It truly is a "jam" as everyone listens and shares. No topics are "off the table."

Be prepared. This exciting phase of Brand Re-Engineering will surprise, encourage, challenge, and enlighten. It will determine where best to place your focus based on timeframe, resources, and opportunity (perhaps there is an upcoming industry event or a new product to launch). It's time to allow what has been discovered to influence the future.

The following is the story of how a small, Midwestern company re-engineered its brand to be a powerful presence in its industry.

Hungry to Grow

Strataflo Products competed against multinational companies that positioned themselves as low-cost leaders. Possessing an impressive ability to design and produce high-quality valves, this team could accomplish anything humanly possible with a valve, and they could do it now. However, they were not top of mind in the industry, sometimes pigeonholed as folksy and small, certainly not a formidable competitor. This limited their opportunities to bid on projects, both large and small. Their president, Andy Warner, was committed to changing that.

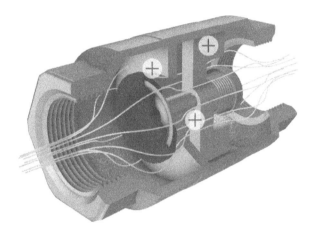

Our team began by guiding the process of uncovering Strataflo's differentiators. We discovered their unique ability to engineer and manufacture high-quality, solution-based products utilizing their technology and expertise. That story needed to be shared, and Strataflo's website became the vehicle for doing exactly that.

At the time, their website was basic and spartan: a carousel of products with little personality or uniqueness. However, this was a team with great passion and extraordinary talent, and that story needed to be told. As we looked at their competitors' sites, which were filled with sterile images of products, specifications, and facilities, we saw an opportunity for Strataflo to stand out. We "humanized" the brand's image by featuring their proud engineering and manufacturing teams in action.

Next, Andy shared his vision of being able to sell Strataflo valves online, including their patented modular check valve product that allows customers to select the best valve configuration for their system. We developed a robust e-commerce solution, including a "valve builder" that guided customers through the process of configuring their specific valves. This simple, easy-to-use tool was unlike the far more cumbersome and clumsy tools offered by their competitors. The valve builder positioned them as a leader in the market, far more advanced and customized than their traditional, stale competition.

Andy, being the leader of a small, well-run company, had to ensure smart investments in the brand, as he certainly did not have a limitless budget. That meant making tough decisions by reducing the budget elsewhere. For example, underperforming trade shows and a handful of "nice-to-do" but non-critical projects were canceled or reduced to maximize their existing budget.

Andy and his tight-knit team made great strides as they welcomed new customers by promoting their creative design abilities. Their pricing inched up as well. Each year, we "jam" with Andy on where to take the brand next and focus the budget on those areas.

Today, customers and employees better recognize the uniqueness and value of Strataflo. The competition may be multinational, but none are more entrepreneurial or able to design amazing solution-based valves like they do.

Your Brand Strategy Roadmap will arm you with an inspiring vision of your differentiation and will provide a path for your brand. Next, it's time to execute deliverables and messaging.

CHAPTER 13

STEP 4: BRAND EXECUTION AND DELIVERABLES

NEXT, EVERYTHING DISCOVERED during your Brand Re-Engineering process is applied to the development of your deliverables. This is a step that's unique for every brand. For example, some of our clients' logos are already strong and require no attention, while others may need a minor refresh or new identity altogether. The same goes for taglines. It's all on a case-by-case basis. Keep in mind, if you already have an established logo and tagline, there needs to be a solid case to change them.

In upcoming chapters, I'll cover photography, videography, technology, and training executions that bring a brand to life. I've chosen here to focus on the importance and power of *words*. I cannot emphasize strongly enough how important your brand language or *lexicon* is, as it should be woven into every message and communication you make.

Once you have mastered your lexicon, it must be faithfully and consistently applied to social media, videos, training, websites, and marketing campaigns.

200,000 Words

I'm a stickler (or maybe a "pain" is a better word) when it comes to words. As an example, let's face it, most taglines or slogans are useless. They try to say so much yet end up meaning nothing as we pay no attention to them. Fight the temptation to create a slogan that sounds cute or clever. Never, ever use a cliché.

Approximately 200,000 words are in the English language. That means there are plenty of opportunities to discover the right term or phrases in describing your differentiation and brand. As Abraham Joshua Heschel said, "Words create worlds." Your goal is to find the exact language that sets you apart from the crowd. Even if you fall a little short, you're ahead of the pack that is producing uninteresting pablum for the world to digest.

Two Words Made the Difference Between Success and Failure

My team was hired by a healthcare furniture manufacturer. Their energetic president and founder told us, "I'm excited for you to learn about us and our brilliant design."

We conducted their Brand Assessment, asking distributors, customers, and employees what made the brand unique. We heard interesting and somewhat shocking responses.

Employees in the plant uniformly shared, "The product is strong, but our design is terrible. It's embarrassing." Distributors spoke up, "They're great people to work with but are way behind the industry in design." Customers chimed in, "We order their chairs even though they look very old and outdated."

Despite these critical comments, or maybe because of them, our team was excited, knowing there must be a story behind this, as the company had been successful and was highly respected. Continuing to investigate, we found an emerging narrative that would explain everything. It was all about one word: design.

Several weeks later, we met with the president and team to discuss the findings, preparing him to be surprised but asking him to first exhale and relax. I then covered the comments we heard regarding their lackluster design. There was no way to put a spin on the weakness. His face turned red; his blood pressure was surely rising.

The president glanced around the room at his leaders, hoping to hear disagreement on what I had shared so far. There was none. One executive turned his attention to the president, "I've been saying this for years. Our design is terrible. Maybe you'll listen to us now." The president took a deep breath and spoke up. "You're giving me a heart attack. This is not what I expected to hear."

I then discussed that while their design was lacking, there was good news in all of this, as his customers, dealers, and employees uniformly agreed the brand had one extraordinary strength that made up for it. "Everyone interviewed felt your engineering is not simply good, it is genius. That brilliant engineering allows for easy assembly and seamless fabric replacement, which is a huge advantage in the healthcare industry." The president was stunned. "So, all along, I've been pounding my fist to make sure we trumpet our design in every ad and every speech I make. That message must have been a disconnect. I've always looked at *engineering* and *design* as being the same thing. Evidently, I've been alone in that assumption."

Words do create worlds. Claiming to be a design leader, while most viewed them as dated and old school, made the brand look out of touch and allowed the competition to gain ground. This moment was a milestone for the team as they now realized who they were and moved forward celebrating and promoting their engineering differentiation. To the president's credit, he didn't just accept that their design needed work, he updated and modernized it to further enhance the industry-leading brand.

We're Not Tree Huggers

We helped a distributor in the environmental services industry discover and differentiate its brand. That relationship started with a surprising admission from their leader. "We are not tree huggers," Daphne replied in her husky voice. She was a colorful character. Her employees knew the familiar roar of her motorcycle as well as her well-chronicled ability to party until sunrise. She had been her father's right hand and had taken over the company after his recent passing.

Before it's assumed that Daphne was the wild child of the family, let's make this clear: "Daddy" was the Keith Richards of their industry. No one could keep up with his lifestyle or his charity. If you were a customer and needed a part for your truck, he'd say, "No problem. Pick it up and don't worry about paying for it—you're good. Send me the money when you're ready."

Unfortunately, when Daphne's dad passed away, it left her with a complex mess. No systems, no records of who owed what, and enormous debt. She desperately needed to refocus the company.

One day, Daphne fessed up. "I don't give a [hoot] about the environment. None of us here do. I mean, I don't hate it, but I want to drink water from a plastic bottle if I feel like it." She said this sincerely and with just a hint of defiance.

She continued. "Here's what we love—we love to help the people out there who are digging holes, putting in systems, and installing stuff. They need someone to trust who knows the equipment and can service it any time they need it. That's where we come in." Her sentiments reflected what her people and customers said. They loved to serve.

She offered up one more insight (it was more of a warning) before we began working together. "A few years ago, a fancy consultant came in and told us to create some corporately correct mission statement saying we were here to save the planet and all that [crap]. But that wasn't us. Employees thought it was stupid. We still laugh about that. It was a disaster! It wasn't who we are, and it set us back."

This is typical when companies try to adopt generic core values that sound good. But they are just words—nice, appropriate words and clichés that mean nothing. Daphne ran her company with heart and a dedication to customers. Her brand needed to reflect and celebrate that steadfastness.

Throughout our interviews with employees and customers, her description of the company was reinforced that while they were not "tree huggers," they were certainly not anti-environment, either. Her team was answering the call in the middle of the night and dispatching people to a hazardous spill site to lend a hand. They were driving for hours to repair machinery needed to maintain a municipality's water supply. The company deeply cared for and respected their customers.

One day while chatting, I asked her to consider this as a description of who they are, "*You protect the people who protect our environment.*" She laughed and smiled. "Now that's something I can stand behind because that's us. We love all those service people who are cleaning up the spills and messes, and we're there for them, no matter what, day or night." Her emotions overwhelmed her. "This is who we are, and we can live up to this, proudly, every day. It takes the pressure off trying to be something we're not."

Their mantra became part of their brand's lexicon; it was a point of pride and clarification as to who they were, freeing them to be true to themselves as they served those who protect our environment. And it gave Daphne and her team the license to drink water from a plastic bottle now and then.

Time to Retire the Trope

I hate clichés. I hope to influence you to feel the same. While they may feel comfortable, they usually mean nothing and get no attention, even if they are somewhat true. "World-class," "One-stop shop," "We do it all," "We go the extra mile," "We've got you covered," or "We provide solutions," are just a few examples to run far away from.

According to Wiki:

> A cliché (\ˈklē-shā, kli-ˈshā\) is an expression, idea, or element of an artistic work [that] has become overused to the point of losing its original meaning or effect, even to the point of being trite or irritating, especially when at some earlier time it was meaningful or novel.

Here is an example of a cliché that was once powerful but then lost all value:

A distributor had endured deteriorating market share over its four decades and had installed a new CEO. Since its founding, their slogan was "We Service What We Sell." After I questioned whether that slogan was still relevant, he was defensive. "I see no reason to change it. It's still true today, so why consider creating a new one?"

That was very logical and made some sense. But true to the above definition of cliché, the phrase had become overused to the point that it lost its impact. It no longer meant anything despite it having been a powerful statement forty years ago when they were the rare company with expertise to repair the equipment they sold.

But over the years, it became commonplace for certified distributors or dealers to manage warranty claims and perform repairs as part of their agreements with the brands they represent.

This distributor had been promoting something that was now an expectation of their customers. It had become meaningless and ho-hum. I cover the rest of this brand's story elsewhere in this book and will spare the details, but will say they replaced their old, cliché slogan with a meaningful, inspirational, and relevant rally cry.

Beware of using words like *quality*, *service*, or *value* in your messaging, whether in advertising or mission statements.

The word *value* originally described something of high quality. Today, it means next to nothing because customers can choose entry-level value, high value, or premium value. I've witnessed clients getting into arguments over whether or not they were a "value brand" all because of how confusing the term has become. Challenge yourself to push forward and find better words.

Make sure you *avoid your competitors' lexicon.* Steer clear of their terms and jargon because you'll merely reinforce their brand. To preserve and protect your identity, you need to be fully aware of your competition's words, and refrain from stepping into their territory.

For example, your competitor may *own* the term "advanced." Their slogan could be "Advanced Technology." If so, use words like *innovative or sophisticated,* instead. Claim your territory and avoid theirs when at all possible.

When in Doubt, Leave It Out

Mark Twain wrote, "I didn't have time to write a short letter, so I wrote a long one instead." Your brand messaging must be as elegant as possible using the fewest words to tell your story. As Twain alluded, in my experience, it takes far longer to edit and refine a message than it did to create the first, inspired draft. My mantra is *when in doubt, leave it out*—create messaging that is succinct, clear, and moving. That applies to your slogan, social media, ads, and website copy. It takes time, but your brand deserves it.

Bandwidth

We were approached by a prestigious law firm with a rich history spanning over a century. Despite their esteemed reputation, they faced challenges as they competed against competitors positioning themselves as younger, trendier, and more affordable. Tasked with rejuvenating their brand, we embarked on a comprehensive brand discovery.

To gain a deep understanding of the firm's success over the decades, we conducted interviews with numerous employees and clients. Through these conversations, we uncovered a revelation that would shape their new identity. Repeatedly, we heard about the firm's ability to provide extensive services and expertise to their clients, offering them something unique: bandwidth.

It was a eureka moment for us. This exceptional law firm offered an unparalleled range of legal specialties, including employment, trademark, real estate, and more. When engaging their services, clients gained access to a diverse array of legal expertise, far superior to hiring multiple, smaller firms. The concept of "bandwidth" perfectly encapsulated this differentiating factor. We ensured that this powerful term became an integral part of their messaging, solidifying their ownership of it, while their competitors wisely avoided using it.

In addition to reshaping their messaging, we also addressed their visual identity. Despite being a firm with great diversity, this aspect was not adequately reflected in their marketing materials. Moving forward, we made it a priority to position them as a modern, advanced, and more youthful law firm, presenting their diverse team in advertisements and on social media.

While still being true to who they were, this brilliant law firm repositioned itself to be every bit as relevant and modern as their competition.

Tone

The personality of your brand is critical. Your brand guidelines should include guidance in this area. Is your brand confident, arrogant, or are you positioned as a friendly and knowledgeable expert? If you are a Germanic high-tech brand, you might employ a precise style of verbiage that is more on the technical side. If you are a proud motorcycle icon, you would employ an edgy, "in your face" approach with bravado.

Elevator Speech

Once you discover your differentiation, the creation of an elevator speech is powerful. It's a two-to-four-sentence description of what you do or what your brand is all about. Share yours with the team, but don't require them to memorize it verbatim because it will sound stiff and robotic.

Helping Volvo Cars relaunch their brand and spread the word, we conducted elevator speech classes for thousands of dealer personnel.

Key to this was ensuring that each person created and shared their personal, genuine version. Soon there were thousands of consistent, but authentically sincere Volvo elevator speeches being shared nationwide.

Doctors, engineers, CEOs, receptionists, and dog groomers all need to explain to their friends, family, co-workers, and customers why they do what they do. Here's a great elevator speech from one of the nation's leading wealth management experts, Mike Palmer. "A lot of wealth managers say they want to take their client from 'Point A to Point B.' That involves too much risk. I focus on the client who's worked their entire life to get to 'Point B' and wants to preserve that wealth. I make sure they're protected and don't put their well-earned wealth at risk." *Your elevator speech is not a work of art; it's a work from the heart.*

Your Story

Telling your story is a popular business topic today. But, as mentioned regarding clichés and overused words, make sure it's meaningful and that your differentiation is the "star." If you're merely reciting a company timeline or giving a history lesson, you're putting people to sleep.

Make it interesting. Do we want to hear about how you were founded in 1983, have three hundred employees, build ambulances, and then list the machines and various people that work there? Or do we capture attention by sharing that *forty years ago, three paramedics joined forces to build lifesaving vehicles. Each unit saves or protects over 100,000 occupants over its lifespan, meaning we've helped protect millions of lives with our technology over the years. Plus, half of the people in our plant are volunteer firefighters. Safety is in our DNA.*

Customers, employees, and employees' families will rally around an interesting story that focuses on what gives you and the brand a true meaning.

Choosing your brand's lexicon is critical in setting it apart from the competition as well as attracting and motivating your employees and customers. Avoiding clichés and instead selecting the precise words you can "own" will help you differentiate. After all, there are 200,000 to choose from.

CHAPTER 14

STEP 5: INTERNAL LAUNCH AND (ULTIMATELY) EXTERNAL LAUNCH

WHY DOES MY COMPANY INSIST our clients launch their new branding and messaging to employees before anyone else in the world knows about it? The answer to that question lies in this true story that has been altered to protect the innocent.

Following months of focus and enormous investment, a company launched its new brand: a refreshed website, social media campaigns, trade advertising, and digital marketing. The phone rings at headquarters and a receptionist answers. "Hello, Acme Worldwide. Our new campaign? We have a new campaign? No, I don't know anything about the product you're asking about. The powers that be don't tell us anything. Hello? Hello. . .? Hmm. . . Must've hung up."

In my four decades of serving great clients and brands, I have seen this scenario take place more times than you might imagine—good companies with ambitious goals investing massively to launch a product, yet neglecting to involve the people who build it, service it, sell it, or support it.

I used to get pushback trying to convince clients to share their vision and differentiation with their employees *first* before they launched the product. I'd often hear something like, "Why waste time and money telling our people all that stuff? They need to keep their heads down and push units out the door." Fortunately, the world has changed, and that archaic thinking is withering away.

A leader's responsibility is to help their people understand that what they are doing will make the world better. If employees deeply believe they are helping to save lives with the fire truck they're manufacturing, maybe they won't leave to take the job at the marshmallow factory across town for fifty cents an hour more.

You may employ one dozen or four thousand employees to make a product or provide a service. Often, they are only involved in one part of the process and do not understand the brand, what makes it unique, or the brilliance behind its design. Seldom are they encouraged or allowed to meet the end user. Imagine the challenge of connecting what they do with who they do it for. As leaders, that's our challenge as well, and we can eliminate that disconnect.

Walk a Mile in Your Customers' Shoes

Astute business executives oversaw a mobility van company. A mobility vehicle is a retrofitted van that has a ramp and other equipment installed to allow a person in a wheelchair to enter and operate it. While to many of us this sounds like an unexciting product, to the person in a wheelchair it represents freedom to shop, go to events, or visit their doctor. It's their lifeline to the world.

The company executives were well-educated, schooled in accounting, Six Sigma, and engineering. However, morale throughout the organization was at rock bottom. Product quality and market share were diminishing. They were, at the time, a "me-too" product, in second place competing against a tough, historically dominant competitor.

One afternoon, I joined a leadership team meeting as they discussed the serious quality issues in front of them. I could sense the frustration in the room as they pored over the latest data showing that each unit averaged well over one dozen flaws. Often, those issues were minor: loose bolts, torn carpeting, or metal shavings left inside the glove box. That made it all the more frustrating because these could be easily overcome, it seemed. The executives were convinced the people in their plant didn't care and that the Six Sigma process was not working.

I suggested the leaders walk downstairs to the factory floor and inspect the vans themselves to demonstrate how much it mattered. That notion was rejected immediately. "We hired people for that." Their response confirmed what we had uncovered in our brand assessment: Employees and dealers perceived that leadership didn't care about quality, customers, or their people; rather, their only focus was on making money. It seemed clear that if they didn't take time to personally inspect units, the quality of the workmanship wasn't all that important to them. If true, why should the employees care? But hope endured as we helped our clients *walk in their customers' shoes.*

Their customers were disabled people who would maneuver (in a wheelchair) into the van, position themselves, and then drive it using ingenious technology created by the company. The van was not just a vehicle to the owner. It connected them to the world and had to be functional and dependable. It could not break down without potentially dire consequences.

One customer interview I conducted illustrated the importance of product quality. She told me, "You have to realize what it means for me to own my van. It gives me some semblance of a normal life. It's amazing. But you must also understand that for a person confined to a chair, if the ramp doesn't deploy and I'm stuck in there, it's frightening. The thought of crawling from the chair and trying to somehow climb out of the van when the ground below looks like the Grand Canyon is terrifying."

I shared this story with leadership to move them, to touch their humanity so they could realize the impact their product made. *They weren't just converting a vehicle to be wheelchair accessible; their van was an integral part of their customers' lives. When it worked, it was a godsend. When it didn't, it was a nightmare.*

Since the leadership hadn't fully appreciated this, then neither could their three hundred employees. To their credit, they knew it was time for a wakeup call. The CEO became energized, collaborating with us to create an extraordinary employee experience celebrating the brand and thanking them for making a difference in so many lives.

Armed with the brand differentiation we learned from our Technical Immersion and the passion of the revitalized executive team, we invited employees to celebrate their contributions by experiencing a once-in-a-lifetime event. And, now with the leaders' support, this wasn't just a company meeting at the plant. It would entail all employees boarding a bus to a secret location for the day (the CEO's idea). The location? Where would you hold a celebration for a mobility van manufacturer? At a racetrack, of course! In addition to racing the vans around the oval with professional drivers at the wheel, we had a few more surprises planned.

Before I share more, here's an illustration of just how far the CEO had progressed throughout this process. While his leadership team was supportive of this event, they did push back on shutting down the entire plant for the day. They suggested, instead, two half-day events be held with 150 employees attending while the others remained working to allow production to continue. Impressively, he flatly rejected the idea. "We're not going to build up our team if we cut it in half. We're making the commitment; we're doing it right." Kudos to him for standing up against a convenient and efficient but less inspiring concept. This powerfully demonstrated his passion. I must admit, I learned from him in this instance; I would have been tempted to follow his team's recommendation.

All three hundred employees were transported to the motor speedway. Excitement was in the air, as many of them had attended NASCAR and other events there. They arrived to find wheelchairs placed in front of their entire fleet of products. Each employee was then asked to sit in a wheelchair and experience what it was like to roll up the ramp, maneuver a 360-degree turn inside the van, then try to position themselves to drive. Few had even seen the final product before it left the plant; now they were playing the role of a customer.

As you might guess, many were fumbling around trying to maneuver. That experience alone enlightened each of them as to what their customers had already mastered.

Next, the employees participated in a competitive comparison experience. The CEO invested serious money to rent the units of their top competitors, which wasn't a cheap or easy thing to do, but it paid off. Employees could examine the competition's construction quality, features, and technologies. The team's proud sales force informed employees of the advantages and differentiation of their brand. Then came one more surprise.

The CEO gathered employees in the racetrack stands and announced that two special guests were about to join the celebration. I could hear voices whispering in the crowd, wondering if it was a politician or a famous race car driver who was about to step up to the podium. But no one "stepped up."

Coming from behind the stage, two long-time customers rolled up in their wheelchairs as they were greeted to a standing ovation from employees. For the next ten minutes, the CEO interviewed them on their lives, how they came to be in their wheelchairs, what it was like to experience the world as they did, and the role their mobility van played in their lives. One customer had been a gifted athlete who was injured playing pickup baseball with friends. The other had contracted polio as a young man and never recovered from the paralysis. In each case, their spirit and energy were inspiring and, for all of us witnessing it, you simply could not walk away without being in awe of how they had been able to lead their lives. There wasn't a dry eye in the crowd.

Employees left the day fully understanding their role and the value of their brand. They now knew, loved, and admired their customers. Immediately following our event, the brand's quality metrics began skyrocketing. Soon, the leadership shared their annual employee survey results with me. Satisfaction with leadership rose from 25 percent the previous year to 94 percent.

Without either pay increases or brand-new quality processes, this rejuvenated team performed at the highest level in their history. All that extraordinary progress was accomplished because leadership peered into the mirror and realized they needed to show they cared. Employees connected with the customer and product, understanding the crucial role they play in helping amazing human beings live their lives to the fullest.

How well do your employees know your customer? How much of a difference do they feel they make? Do they feel you really care? I hope you apply this to your brand and team. This story is one of over one hundred we have been involved with throughout the world and in each situation, they were rewarding, motivational experiences, remembered and valued for a lifetime.

Tips on Creating the Most Inspiring Internal Brand Launch

Take the Time

Shutting down an operation is expensive but rushing through a meaningless meeting is completely wasteful. If it's a full day, half day, or a forty-five-minute meeting, give it your full focus by sharing the exciting news about the company, brand, and differentiation with the people who most influence your product or service: your employees. Don't cut corners.

Inform Everyone in the Enterprise

At Betts Industries, a 120-year-old component manufacturer, Michelle Betts conducted brand celebrations with each of their three shifts on the same day and night to ensure everyone understood how valuable they were to the company. We provided the materials for Michelle to present, but it was all on her shoulders, and she came through with flying colors, exhausted but satisfied their employees' contributions were honored.

Consider a Virtual or Hybrid Event

SDI LaFarga COPPERWORKS conducted a virtual Internal Launch for their one hundred team members. They shipped a brand launch package in advance to all employees containing gifts that proudly displayed their new logo and identity, including a custom COPPERWORKS-branded beer, hat, and water bottle. All from their plant, as well as executives elsewhere in the world, shared in the exciting celebration.

Decades ago, before today's world of virtual meetings, we conducted a global Internal Launch for Volkswagen via satellite. Looking back, it's mindboggling how difficult and complex that was. Today, it's easier, less expensive, and well worth considering going virtual.

Leverage Your Event

Use this as an opportunity to rally employees to clean up, organize, and rebrand your facility. One of our clients unleashed their team to repaint their entire factory and erect signage for each assembly station prior to an internal branding celebration. The improvement was amazing, resulting in an uplifting experience not only for employees but for visitors and customers, as well.

Avoid the Void by Addressing the Invisible Elephants

Employees usually sense if things are going poorly or if there are issues at the company. Don't be the leader who avoids addressing them, as people will most likely assume the worst. All of us will fill that void of information with negativity. *Avoid the void* and speak the truth. Give the team confidence in your leadership.

When we helped Volkswagen conduct an Internal Launch with their team, leader Len Hunt took the wise and bold step to be transparent with them. There had been rumblings of a potential layoff due to economic conditions. Instead of sidestepping the issue, Len spoke from his heart and acknowledged that it could be a reality but added, "While this is possible, you can trust that I will fight it every step of the way. You have my word." Len's courage and candor comforted employees, and perhaps because of their elevated performance moving forward, Len was able to avoid any staff reduction.

Tell Your World

Share with your employees first, but since you have already invested time and resources, why not also ask dealers, suppliers, or local press to join in the celebration later that day? Also, consider inviting employees and families for lunch or dinner at the facility to allow them to share in the excitement. John, Bohn, and Chris Popp, owners of Aunt Millie's Bakeries, sponsored picnics for employees and families at their facilities to honor the hard work and dedication of the team. This smart and compassionate gesture let their employees know the Popp family truly cares.

Entertain

In the world of wealth management, Oxford Financial Group is held in the highest regard. When founder and CEO Jeff Thomasson gathered his team together in Indianapolis to share and celebrate their new and improved branding, he surprised everyone. Jeff, well known as a genius and visionary in the world of wealth management, proudly introduced their keynote speaker as a "globally renowned industry expert." The audience was on the edge of their seats to hear the brilliance that was to come.

Jeff then sat back as the speaker launched into a half-hour comedy sketch, sometimes poking lighthearted fun at the expense of him and his team. As the audience slowly realized "this guy is actually a professional comedian, where everything he said was 'double talk' and nothing made sense," it served as a brilliant, well-deserved break in the action during an otherwise serious, focused meeting. Years later, the performance is still remembered fondly. Jeff illustrated that he understood and cared for his team, giving them a chance to relax and enjoy the moment.

Focus Your Message

Critical to any successful Internal Launch is your message. It's important that the focus is on the brand, your differentiation, and how employees played a role in the discovery process. Share quotes from satisfied dealers and customers that support that narrative. Please, no discussion of stock price or profit (unless everyone is sharing in them). This is your best chance to provide meaning to your employees, giving them legitimate pride in what they do.

When FreightCar America Chairman Jim Meyer spoke to his employees shortly after the company invested substantially in their facility, he focused on a profound message that rang true with them: their safety. While Jim had steered the company to their first profitable quarter in years, he didn't discuss stock price or shareholder return. Instead, he shared the new investment in equipment that ensured a safer environment. From an employee's standpoint, it's far more meaningful to know your leader cares about your health rather than an uptick in the company's stock price.

Make It Authentic

In Australia, a mining company organized an Internal Launch and, to commemorate their new branding, invited employees to pose for photos standing on top of one of their giant-sized mining implements. At Volkswagen's release of the New Beetle, the company erected a photo station where employees could stand behind a cardboard cutout of the product, posing as if they were crammed inside it. Every company has its own personality. Enjoy, and have fun.

Tell Employees First

This event may be your chance to give employees a sneak peek at the future. If possible, share a new product or service you have not yet announced to the world. Len Hunt, while leading Volkswagen, had a bold inspiration: *Why not give employees a first look at our new product before the automotive press sees it?* Historically, auto manufacturers reveal their new product at a global trade show, after which employees would learn about it. Instead, at the Volkswagen Internal Launch, Len asked everyone to put their cell phones down as he rolled out the new product for them to see and touch. Never in their lives would his employees have expected that opportunity. There was a mad dash to the new car, and no one pulled out their cell phone. Len won a lot of fans that day.

Invite Special Guests

Consider this if you want to make an incredible impact. Prior to your event, share the news that "special guests" will join the celebration to say a few words to the employees. Usually, employees will assume a company executive or board member will address them. Surprise everyone with the most meaningful guests imaginable—your loyal customers. Think of the self-respect all will feel when they see and hear from the customer just how great their product or service is and what a difference it makes in their lives. No kidding, you will see people beaming with pride.

Do It!

As I have shared many times, it's not about being perfect—it's about sharing the progress being made; it's about showing you value your employees above all. So, you don't have a huge budget or a fancy presentation, and don't have a new product to launch? No worries, get out there and show your team you believe in them.

We focused on the Internal Launch in this chapter. After a successful internal celebration, the rest of the world should then be included. Think next of those closest to your enterprise, including suppliers, dealers, distributors, and key customers. They deserve an early look at where you are going, since they influenced it. This will drive even more loyalty and better performance.

After that, it's time to tell the world, knowing your enterprise will be ready to represent your new image and messaging to maximize your investment.

CHAPTER 15

LET'S JAM!

"JAMMING" IS BOTH A CORE VALUE and a differentiator for our firm. A LABOV Jam Session™ is our proprietary process of listening, collaboration, ideation, and team building designed to result in uplifting, *actionable* concepts. This is a way of life for our company as we conduct—with clients as well as internally—hundreds of these collaborations a year to generate breakthrough thinking.

A Jam Session is a tool to help tackle our clients' challenges and opportunities. We invite their "entire band" to join in, including executives and their sales, engineering, customer service, and marketing teams. Everyone has a voice.

Throughout this special day, we focus on creating concepts that are inspiring and can be realistically achieved by the organization. We've helped companies relaunch their brands, create groundbreaking marketing programs, devise new service offerings to overcome marketplace competition, and other exciting challenges.

We employ Adult Learning Principles, which include creating a safe environment to express yourself, providing variety with small teams (three to five participants) as well as entire group collaboration, and ensuring it is fast paced with no activity lasting longer than 45 minutes. For clients, the experience will fly by quickly and seamlessly.

For my team, it is a choreographed performance that is uniquely rewarding for the audience.

The LABOV Jam team is led by Account Supervisor, Sal Farias. Sal's passion for people and camaraderie are key in making our jams productive and positive experiences. Joining him as his jam partner is "bandmate" Sara Petrie who has a gift for leading and engaging people. Here's how we orchestrate a Jam Session:

1. Pre-Work

One week prior to the session, we ask participants to submit their strongest three solutions to the challenge we're tackling, such as identifying your unique differentiators or creating a brand-new service offering. They digitally send their ideas to us prior to the session. This step creates engagement and momentum *before* the jam begins. Depending on the size of the audience, we will receive thirty to fifty ideas or more. While the majority are just basic "thoughts," they serve as a foundation for the collaborative ideation to come. Then, it's time to attend the jam!

2. "We're the Beach Crüe!"

As they arrive, participants are assigned to small table teams of usually three to five people. After introducing themselves, they immediately face their first task: naming their team or "band." This generates entertaining discussions regarding each person's favorite performer, from Taylor Swift to Miles Davis to Toby Keith. We've seen some creative names like "Beach Crüe" (a combination of the Beach Boys and Mötley Crüe) and the pandemic-themed "Straight to Quarantine." Teams begin the process of collaborating as they discuss and broker which identity they will be known as for the next six hours or so. This serves as an "icebreaker" and is their first jam of the day.

3. Jamming 101

This is where we explain what a jam is and what the participants should expect from the day, as it will not be a standard meeting. We'll inform everyone that jamming is all about listening: listening to a team member, then responding with your input as others consider your thoughts and do the same. You cannot create without sincerely listening and contemplating what others are saying. This give and take, without judgment, will unleash great thinking.

And we share that it's not about being perfect; it's about experimenting and considering possibilities, allowing new ideas to be considered without immediately filtering or dismissing them. In the corporate world, there is great pressure to avoid mistakes, to be perfect—this experience is fun and a safe place for people to open up and share.

One more point: One of our ground rules for the session is we focus only on what we can affect or influence. No wasting time or energy on politics, the economy, future pandemics, or military conflicts. This allows for a positive, refreshing day for all.

4. Scenarios of Your Future

Here, we will present three future scenarios for your company. This creative "device" allows a person to get out of the moment and safely start their creative juices flowing. After each scenario is presented, the entire group will share their responses. These can lead to powerful revelations as well as interesting ideation. Be forewarned, it's a bit of a roller coaster ride as we explore the fears and hopes of the group.

Our first scenario is not a positive one and is set three years, exactly to that day, in the future. We'll project onto a screen a "mock" headline from a local newspaper or trade magazine. It will represent a concerning, troubling message: *XYZ company loses market share, is now up for sale. Once having a proud future, now searching for a buyer.*

The mood is understandably low as the group contemplates this coming to pass as well as how it would feel if this was reality. The next few minutes is an open dialogue on why and how this happened, exploring what they did and what they did not do that enabled this to take place. Often, people will share how much it would disappoint them if the company fell short. As difficult as this discussion will be, it is ultimately positive as everyone is aware it's not reality and that there are opportunities to make sure it never happens.

Next, we reveal a far more positive headline, again set three years in the future: *XYZ company sees record growth, expanding to new markets, the sky's the limit.* The group responds to why and how it occurred. Their emotions in discussing this usually include pride and confidence. They delve into what was done to accomplish this as well as what they stopped doing. There's a feeling of confidence as the entire group envisions a brighter future. More than just a feel-good moment, this is where the group leverages the failures from the first scenario to steel themselves, moving forward boldly with new resolve. Next, there's a *twist*.

We then unveil a surprising, final, third headline. Unlike the previous two, this is set in the present day: *Leadership group from XYZ company* (the people in this jam session) *takes control and acquires it.* This is a pivotal moment designed for participants to imagine they take full ownership of the situation, no excuses. At that point, we will often hear, "Oh, my gosh" or another expression of surprise.

Usually, an even deeper level of seriousness takes place as all discuss issues and opportunities that now must be focused on. It's a reality check, in that what is concluded is what actually should be going on today. This is a call to action preparing the group to create realistic, actionable concepts throughout the remainder of the session. It sets up the remainder of the day beautifully, turbocharging the intensity.

5. Ideation Begins

Each small table team then reconvenes. They review the *pre-work* they sent prior to the meeting, plus any ideas that were discussed or developed based off the scenario exercises. Each participant shares what they believe in and why. Everyone is listened to, and each idea is given focus and never rejected or judged harshly. It's common for more than a dozen ideas to be shared. And this is where candor, vulnerability, and teamwork take place. Participants not only discuss, but also roll up their sleeves to help others strengthen their concepts.

6. Top Five

Next, the table teams cull the dozens of ideas down to their "Top Five," refining them and getting serious. We guide them to validate and improve each concept by naming it, identifying the audience, exploring how to market it, and predicting the potential value delivered as well as its cost to the enterprise if adopted. At this point, there are exciting interactions and collaborations. Often, several ideas will be combined into a single, superior one. The teams act with an elevated sense of ownership, making sure each of their "Top Five" is as strong as possible.

7. The Hit Parade

Now that your table has determined its "Top Five," we ask you to step away, so other teams can review your work and vote on their favorites. This independent review is cathartic; it allows you to learn what others see in your ideation. And, you'll do the same as you review and vote on the masterpieces created by the other teams. In the end, the top three ideas from each team are identified. Those are the only concepts focused on for the rest of the session, focusing all attention to the best thinking.

To reiterate, you do not vote on your own ideas; others with fresh eyes choose them. Just like in a rock band, you may love the song you wrote, but it's up to the audience to buy the record or not. If they love it, you'll make the Hit Parade! This is critical because often a person will have their own "pet" idea that they fight for. It's human nature to love a concept and constantly push for it, only to be frustrated as it never is realized. Our process eliminates the person and their team voting for that favored concept; it must pass muster with others.

Prior to a Jam Session, a healthcare client confided, "I'm concerned that Molly will fight for an idea she's been pushing for years. It's a point of contention with several of us on the team." Molly did argue for her concept, and with her urging, it was chosen as one of her team's top five ideas. But it did not receive a single vote from the others in the Hit Parade portion of our jam, missing the cut. Her response, "Well, I guess I need to focus on other things. My idea isn't bad, it's just that we, as a team, have stronger ones to dig into." Problem solved.

8. Break Time

Here, we allow everyone to exhale, grab lunch, and learn how to write a song while a band of musicians joins us to perform a real "live" jam. The participants will take part, creating a beat, and picking a "key" (as in the key of G or A) out of a basket for the musicians to play in. Immediately, the entire group is engaged, creating a piece of music that never had existed before. How many times do you write a song at lunch?

Then, after we're refreshed, we all jump back into the session to refine and present the day's ideas.

9. Ship It

We now focus on each team's top three ideas, as voted on during the Hit Parade step. This is where concepts come to life and are fleshed out. Each will be given its own name, slogan, and visual identity. Its target audience will be determined, as will the steps needed to best ensure success. We're compressing a month's worth of ideating in only minutes to create the deepest, most high-impact ideation. There's plenty of listening and volleying of concepts between the teams as they hone and refine each vision for maximum potential. After they've hammered all this out, each team will determine who will present their ideas. Often, it'll require several people working in harmony to position the concept at its strongest. It's time to go on stage and perform.

10. Let's Vote

Each team has finally reached the point where they've listened, collaborated, and then created their top concepts. Now, it's time to present to the entire group and see their reactions.

The Rolling Stones used this technique when they were writing songs for a new album. Before recording them in a studio, they'd evaluate new songs in front of small audiences at local clubs in England. It was eye-opening for them to witness which tunes went over well and which needed more work.

Now, each table team does the same as they share their opuses. There's a little nervousness, but it's fun, and often the entire audience will participate by suggesting tweaks to make ideas even stronger.

After all are presented, the group casts their votes for their favorite. It doesn't matter which one receives the most votes because they are all winners and will soon be presented to the leadership team.

11. Vision of the Future

One of the benefits I have at the company is the ability to use our team's talents in unique ways. Matt Hakey, our Associate Creative Director, and Marcus McMillen, Partner, are tremendous graphic artists, who will create an original "portrait" of the participants' unique vision of their future. This sketch will have been conceived and developed throughout the day as they observe the group, listening to them describe their hopes for the future of the company. Because everyone will have been so involved jamming with their table teams, few will have noticed this had been taking place until it's revealed.

Matt and Marcus share it with all, gain input (sometimes even refine it on the spot), and then ask everyone to sign it. This memorializes the day and deepens the commitment for all. This commemorative masterpiece has often found its place on the walls of our clients' offices. It's an emotional, galvanizing send-off for the group as they leave knowing they accomplished so much in a relatively short period of time. Then, we make sure that these concepts live on.

12. Jam Session Package

We will organize the entire session into a single document, including all concepts, action plans, and photos from the day. Within twenty-four hours, we send our clients this powerful manifesto. It's in their hands and ready to share with decision-makers.

In some cases, our clients' leadership teams have adopted or piloted at least one, often two, Jam Session concepts within forty-eight hours—unheard of speed for most corporations.

Encore Sessions

The success of these experiences has been so powerful that they've given birth to "Encore Sessions," which take place shortly after the initial session itself. Our client will choose two concepts from their Jam to explore even further. Often, these have great potential, but are more complex and require in-depth focus. Encore Sessions are conducted with our small cross-functional teams to allow for quick feedback from all constituents. As with the Jam Sessions, the recommendations are to be shared with decision-makers within forty-eight hours of its conclusion.

Perpetual Ideation

Jam Sessions are transformational one-day experiences. But to truly change the corporate culture, we create year-round ideation, using both Jam Sessions and Encore Sessions to stimulate ongoing, flowing inventiveness, engaging internal as well as external participants such as customers, sales channel, and industry experts.

A Healthier World

Today's healthcare industry is fraught with challenges. Parkview Regional Health CEO Rick Henvey and Dr. Greg Johnson, Regional Market President, are two leaders who have pushed the envelope to re-imagine a healthier world. They were champions and cheerleaders of our Jam Session concept, gathering doctors and administrative leaders to listen, learn, and create a more caring, healthier future for their enterprise and the thousands who represent it.

Jam with James

Worldwide, there are over 5,000 distilled spirits brands. A gin, brandy, rum, vodka, tequila, or whisky label can easily be lost on the shelves of the local grocery or liquor store. James Bowers, leading consultant and advocate in the alcohol and hospitality industries, knows this well. He is also an established recording artist, with several albums to his credit, which explains how he approaches his relationships with supplier-partners. James loves to collaborate. Our team has conducted numerous *Jam with James* sessions, creating dozens of concepts to help better differentiate the spirits brands he represents, which are among the world's most revered. Interestingly, James is not only a fantastic performer, he also plays the role of "producer" in his Jam Sessions, bringing out the very best of everyone.

Steel Guitar

Barry Schneider is not only the President and Chief Operating Officer of Steel Dynamics, but he is also an avid music enthusiast who restores, refurbishes, and refinishes guitars. He often creates his "masterpieces" for friends and business associates. He takes that passion for music and creativity to his team, encouraging them to jam and freely collaborate in order to push further in their engineering and sustainability innovations.

Thinking Outdoors of the Box

Marc-Andre Dubois, or "MAD" as he is affectionately known, is a dynamic visionary. During his tenure at BRP (makers of Can-Am, Sea-Doo, Ski-Doo, and other worldwide brands), he led his team to overcome the pandemic and resulting product shortages. Under his leadership, we facilitated Jam Sessions focusing on two different regions of the U.S. where BRP looked to step up its market share. We engaged a widely diverse group of regional as well as international BRP leaders, producing strategies to propel the brand to dominance in those locales. Several programs born in the jams were initially piloted and later perfected to build market share. Instead of allowing his team to be victims of the pandemic, Marc-Andre Dubois saw it as an opportunity to expand on their differentiation.

The outcomes of a Jam Session include ideation, enhanced team building, and the establishment of new behaviors such as listening and, of course, collaboration.

CHAPTER 16

SHOWCASE YOUR UNIQUENESS THROUGH MEDIA AND TECHNOLOGY

WE'VE COVERED THE POWER of discovering and celebrating your differentiation. It's time to bring your brand to life. In this and upcoming chapters, I'll be far more granular, sharing insights and secrets in the world of execution. View this as a textbook-like approach, starting here with photography, video, and technology, which are far more than just capturing an image, filmmaking or programming an app, as you'll soon read.

The following are guidelines for each execution to make the most impact. Here are recommendations for creating images that enhance your brand.

Branded Photography

Strike a Pose

Ensure the brand's personality and tone are reflected in all images, starting with your leaders, because to many, they are the brand. Today, dress codes are more relaxed, and executives are usually best portrayed as accessible. The image of a scowling "tough guy" executive is becoming passé. If your brand is inclusive and fun, position leaders likewise, smiling and looking receptive. Consider asking your leaders to wear the brand's apparel, which is exactly how Harley-Davidson executives wisely present themselves in their imagery.

Beauty

A snapshot of your new product on a smartphone is, well, usually just that, a snapshot. However, if your product is stunning, it deserves to be captured professionally at the highest resolution.

Toughness

If your brand's differentiation lies in durability, it's crucial that your product images embody that essence. The strategic use of harsher lighting and grainier textures can significantly reinforce the message. We have the privilege of partnering with a company that manufactures vehicles designed to excel in the most challenging conditions. Our Technical Immersion Leader, Pete Piekarski, who is also an extraordinary graphic artist, ensures that every shot of their product in brochures or on the website accentuates that unique selling point through the application of specialized filters and post-processing effects. Pete protects their positioning by ensuring their photography honors that.

Background

Attention spans are growing shorter by the day—more reason to avoid distracting your audience with random visual "noise" in the background. Take extra effort to position your product as the focal point.

Dust It Off

Your brand needs to look as ideal as possible. That means no dirt, dust, scratches, or imperfections. When an orthopedic implant manufacturer conducted a training program and shared images of it with me, my eyes immediately focused on dust that was captured on their product in numerous photos. This unspoken message was loud and clear: they had low attention to detail. Simply put, if it is not in pristine condition, do not shoot your product until it is.

Render It

Some features and technologies are difficult or impossible to capture in photos. Go digital to create that image. Our client's brand was feverishly preparing for the most important launch in its history. Everything had to be right, which meant there were countless revisions to the product as it was being designed and manufactured. The challenge was that their dealer launch coincided with the day their very first unit was to come off the line. We turned to technology to solve this.

Usually, our clients will provide us a small fleet of new units in advance of a launch to photograph for promotional purposes, such as websites and brochures. In this case, there would be no product available whatsoever. So, with the assistance of their engineers who provided CAD files, our technology team created a gorgeous, digitally rendered unit, that honestly, was slightly more beautiful than the real one! That digital version became the star of their marketing campaigns and website. This technology also enabled the unit to swivel and turn on their website, revealing various features under, as well as inside, the product. It was fascinating to compare the "real thing" to our digital version as the dealers and customers couldn't tell the difference.

Be Accidental

When portraying your people in action, avoid the "mugging for camera" shots with them looking like they know they're in a photo shoot. It should appear they didn't realize they were on camera, which will provide a natural, appealing appearance.

Take Extra

Any photo shoot is part science, part art. Do not skimp. If it took ten attempts to get an excellent shot, try for more in case you capture "magic." You can always press delete later.

Uniformity

It's important to consider not only the executive but also the employee dress code for your shoots. We recommend the team wear attire that proudly displays the brand, nothing extravagant. For manufacturing plant employees, it could simply be a T-shirt bearing your logo. Please avoid shooting photos of factory workers who are dressed as if they were either going to a heavy metal concert or nightclub.

Keep in mind that no customer is inspired by the image of a dirty, ragtag gang cobbling together your product. More likely, they imagine a team in lab coats meticulously assembling a piece of art. Help make that vision possible!

Is the Camera Ready?

All equipment—from the camera to lighting set-up–must function, so check it and look at initial shots to ensure quality. Decades ago, I was at a shoot where the photographer caught an impressive shot of the product performing an amazing feat. Moments later, after everyone left, he confided he had forgotten to load film in the camera and missed the shot. Fortunately, today, with digital photography, that doesn't happen, but malfunctions still do, so check.

Branded Video

Be Dramatic

Rather than producing a brand video that is nothing more than a typical sales pitch, why not infuse it with a touch of personality or drama? Consider featuring your loyal customers as stars of the video. By minimizing self-promotion and instead making the end-user the focal point, you can craft a compelling narrative that will resonate deeply and have a more profound affect than a conventional sales pitch.

Can You Hear Me?

The number one flaw in corporate videos is the audio quality, or lack thereof. Confirm the audio is clear, loud (no "hiss"), and eliminate any distracting background noises. Make sure the microphone is near the subject's mouth. A "boom mic" from across the room will not suffice because it will pick up the strange, muffled effect of sound waves bouncing off the walls.

Voice Performance

Once you know the microphone is capturing clear audio, turn to the performance, which must be genuine, interesting, and natural. Someone merely reciting words is not enough. One trick I use when I produce a session is to direct the voice talent to "over act" as they read the script; it helps ramp up warmth and energy.

Visual Performance

On-camera talent must not only sound great but *look the part* or you'll risk losing the viewer's attention. (Is his tie crooked? Why did she wear that dress? Who combed his hair?) Any distraction will diminish your message, so be ultra-picky.

Your Facility

If you are producing a video that displays your plant or location, it must look immaculate. No cluttered, dirty, worn-out building ever inspired a customer. Repaint, touch up, and remember this is "Hollywood," and that's OK. Your favorite TV shows have unrealistically enormous, pristine sets that look "normal" to the viewer. They're staged to create the perfect scene. Do the same.

Animate It

If you need to show the viewer what cannot be seen, use technology to bring it to life. After a manufacturer developed a breakthrough UV

(Ultraviolet Light) disinfection product, they realized they needed to find a way to demonstrate its technology since it was invisible to the human eye. We created a digital simulation of it subduing COVID-19 on a molecular level and displayed it on their website and in video form as well. Their ingenious technology could now be appreciated and capitalized on.

Bite-Size It

Maximize your video investment. Use your beautiful marketing footage in training modules or edit it for social media messaging. With smart planning, you can capture video and repurpose it in multiple formats for customers, employees, social media, training, and other uses.

Screen Shot

If you are shooting high-resolution video, you can also utilize that to "capture" photographic stills. They can be effective but will not necessarily eliminate the need for a professional photo shoot.

Avoid the Yawner

Produce a factory video that you and your employees are proud of. Walmart selected Aunt Millie's Bakeries to be featured in a television campaign. Wisely, the plant chosen for the shoot was their newest and most photogenic. Scores of happy, energetic, and proud employees in Aunt Millie's attire starred in it, portraying an inspiring image of the brand.

Videos are Not One Size Fits All

While it's perfectly fine for lower resolution video to be used for internal training or basic communication, what you stand for must be reflected in your brand video. If you're the premium leader in your segment, your video must be high quality as well. Paying attention to the seemingly insignificant things like the audio quality or the presentation of the employees or CEO will reap benefits. Details make the difference.

Branded Technology

Better than the Real Thing

When the naked eye cannot see your product's brilliance, virtual reality (VR) can be the prescription. Pharmaceutical giant Eli Lilly utilized VR so physicians could visualize their medicine at work in the bloodstream. Surgeons wore headsets as they "traveled" throughout the human body, witnessing Lilly's industry-leading science. This has far more impact than just talking about your innovation and trusting your audience to imagine it.

Virtually Explain It

When your differentiation can't be easily experienced in person, an app can be the ideal answer. Using augmented reality (AR), a fire truck manufacturer was able to demonstrate how its aerial ladder platform could help emergency personnel scale heights in tight, urban settings without needing its outriggers fully extended. While their competitors' trucks were limited in that capacity, their aerial could be operated safely at a full 360 degrees. This feat would have been extraordinarily difficult to demonstrate at trade shows or at customer locations, but through AR technology, firefighters and dealers simply use their smartphones to virtually "park" the new aerial truck in front of any urban location to experience operating the ladder platform in tight spaces. This brilliant use of tech eliminated the need for the brand to invest millions of dollars in a fleet of demonstration trucks to be driven to dealers and customers nationwide.

Overcome Scarcity

What if you don't have enough products to meet customer demand? Airstream trailers are not only icons in their industry, but they are also coveted and sometimes in short supply at dealerships. The challenge was to make Airstream accessible to consumers, everywhere. And make it fun and interactive. Through Web Graphics Library (WebGL) technology, Airstream customers can now experience Airstream's products and features on their website, exploring every ingenious option, even placing the product in virtual environments, such as a campground.

Make Up for "Heaviness"

What if you manufacture a product that's bulky, weighing hundreds or even thousands of pounds, and costly to ship, yet want to launch it to your distributors and customers? Allison Transmission supplied distributors with a two-pound, three-dimensional model of a heavy-duty transmission that when linked to an AR app, would magically reveal the inner workings of the unit. Distributor personnel and customers easily accessed it via smartphone to appreciate their advanced technology.

Spec It Out

Over the last decade, automotive brands have offered consumers the opportunity to design the ideal digital version of their car online. This technology can be applied to many products in all kinds of industries. "Configurators" help customers devise and envision how your product could be perfect for them. Consider it for your offerings.

Consolidate

Don't know where to store all the specs, PDFs, and images of your products? Create a virtual repository. A leading manufacturer organized all product specifications and information into one app, allowing sales reps and customers to review and access them. Because it was on a virtual platform, the company updated the content easily, cheaply, and quickly any time as needed.

Going Mobile

Laptops are great, but today most of us access information on smartphones and tablets. Everything you produce online must be mobile-friendly for quick, easy navigation. The Macallan Scotch team realized their global sales force was constantly on the move, spending little time behind a laptop, so they ensured all training and sales assets were accessible on mobile devices.

Be Creative with Established Technology

You can revolutionize an established technology. My team reimagined the tried-and-true Portable Document Format (PDF), enabling UPS to achieve amazing things with their healthcare newsletter. We wanted to find a way for videos to play within the PDF rather than inserting links that would drive readers to access a browser to view them. After some exploration, we found that by converting the compression rate of the videos, they could be imported into PDF-like images, pushing the limits of the software. This stretching of technology created a much more seamless experience for readers. A representative from Adobe contacted us to learn how we did it!

Increase Sales and Eliminate Errors

For years, a luxury automotive manufacturer used a paper-based ordering system for their most bespoke, customized car. It required dealer salespeople to fill out (by hand) a ten-page ordering document with the customer, then fax it to headquarters across the Atlantic. The manufacturer was disappointed by the product's lackluster sales, blaming the dealers. Dealers, in turn, claimed the product was not of interest to customers and its pricing was far too high. The problem was not the product or the pricing; it was the *lack of technology*, which made for a complex, overwhelming experience fraught with the potential for error.

We replaced this archaic paper-based system with a web-based electronic ordering technology, allowing the customers (with the assistance of the dealership salesperson) to choose stylized features, from gold stitching to a ridiculously loud sound system. Sales boomed and profits shot sky high. It was not only easier for a customer to build their own masterpiece, but now it was also actually fun.

This technology simplified the process for salespeople who previously had avoided offering the product due to its hassle. The manufacturer's frustration with the dealer vanished as sales soared. Another added benefit? Ordering errors were all but eliminated because the customer now selected and approved the purchase, electronically. No more rejected sales with the customer claiming, "I didn't order the purple stitching on the steering wheel!"

Play With It

Your product differentiation is at its most powerful when experienced hands-on. We created a *technology playground* for a nationwide Volvo Cars training launch. Employing fun, engaging activities and games, the concept enabled the participants to experiment and *play* with features such as Bluetooth, navigation, and *infotainment* without the fear of "breaking it."

Sales personnel became so comfortable that they confidently and proudly presented it to customers. Previously in "Don't-break-it" mode, they had been fearful, uncomfortable, and reluctant to even mention, let alone demonstrate, Volvo technology. Making your differentiation accessible and comfortable to the people who represent you will reap great benefits. Today's consumers must be empowered to play and experiment with technology, or you'll risk losing their business and the investment made in your brand. Another great idea is to reconnect with the customer post-purchase to make sure they are fully immersed with the product and to answer any questions. Don't just train the sales force, train the end user.

As you can see, photography, video, and technology offer a world of opportunity to differentiate.

CHAPTER 17

TRAIN YOUR ENTERPRISE ON DIFFERENTIATION

TRAINING IS OFTEN A COMPANY'S RED-HEADED STEPCHILD, financially constrained, and relegated to the marketing, sales, or human resources departments. It deserves far more respect than that. Once a brand discovers its differentiation, it must immediately share it and educate (train) all who have a role in the enterprise.

I find it bizarre that marketing and advertising firms avoid being involved in their clients' training efforts. It seems to make so much sense that the best path to differentiating your brand is through motivating and educating the very people who live it and represent it. And just like Internal Branding, training is extraordinarily cost-effective because it involves reaching your employees and distribution network—far more economical than advertising to strangers across the world.

Maximize learning and development by applying these best practices:

Reach Out to Everybody

Training should not be limited to salespeople or technicians. All in the enterprise can benefit from it, including suppliers, sales channel, and even, yes, your customers. Educate them to understand your brand, help them feel part of something exciting. Hyundai Motors trains all dealership personnel, including service advisors, who are the crucial connection to the customer after a car is purchased. This leading Korean brand makes sure service advisors understand the processes and technology at their disposal as well as the vital role they play in retaining customers and, ultimately, helping them choose their next Sonata or Palisade.

Make It a Game

Adults learn best when they are actively involved in their learning, rather than being lectured to. "Gamification" (as in *game*-ification) is now an integral aspect of every successful training program. The more fun and interesting you make your brand's history, technology, and uniqueness, the more likely your team will proudly share it with others.

Harley-Davidson challenged my company to help their Information Systems Department communicate and train their teams in compliance, worldwide. It was imperative to their leaders that no matter what country or continent a representative lived in, business was conducted at the highest ethical level to reflect and protect that great brand. Usually, this type of training is expected to be somewhat mundane, tedious, and even heavy-handed.

Instead, we made it a game, naming it *Knights of Compliance*. In the spirit of *A Game of Thrones* and *The Lord of the Rings*, our instructional designers created an otherworldly universe of dragons, blood oaths, and castles designed to capture the attention of the participant, engaging them in protecting Harley-Davidson (the "castle") by adhering to critical compliance practices. Thousands of employees worldwide were trained and certified, earning their own knighthood by successfully "graduating" from the program.

Let it be known, far and
wide that

Deborah Smith

is hereby pledged to the
Bar and Shield, declaring
full commitment to adhere
to the Scrolls of Practices
and defense of the King's
Highway of Data and the
fullness of its domain,
henceforth to be called:

"Lady Deborah, Knight of Compliance"

Keep It Fresh

All educational content must constantly be refreshed because your products, services, and customer base evolve over time. At a minimum, require the enterprise to complete the latest training each year so that they remain up to date.

Certify

Want to get people's attention? Require them to pass training modules or tests to be considered "qualified." It may sound tough, but it's smart. Certification is a point of pride, a "bragging right" for the individual as it gives them access to special events and incentives.

A national retailer with eight hundred dealers and four thousand salespeople was planning a major nationwide product launch. We suggested that before inviting all those individuals to attend the two-day training event, they each needed to take and pass testing on the brand's new learning modules. This caught the attention of the retailer's sales force.

The vast majority joined in, including seasoned veterans and recent hires, allowing the training at the events to be more in-depth since everyone now had a stronger foundation of product and brand knowledge. Those who did not have the interest to get certified were not qualified to attend, saving our client hundreds of thousands of dollars in hotel rooms and catering. A big win for everyone!

Competitive Comparison

The strongest, boldest learning programs reveal how your product and brand stand up against the competition. It exhibits confidence and arms your team with powerful information to share your differentiation and brand value. You can achieve this in many ways, from producing basic PDFs that compare product specifications to conducting elaborate events, which I'll share in a later chapter.

Bite-Size Chunks

Remember the irritation of watching a forty-five-minute training video or enduring that ninety-minute college lecture? Well, those days are over—or please make sure they are—for your brand. With today's super-short attention spans, it's smart to create *micro-learning*, ensuring that your training modules are approximately five minutes or less in length. Have a super-complicated product? Instead of a sixty-minute video, break it down into a dozen, easily digestible five-minute modules.

Customer Demographics and Psychographics

Focus on the customer as well as the product or service. Educate your enterprise on their demographics (for example: age, salary, location, or job title) as well as on their *psychographics* (i.e., are they interested in technology or the environment, are they conservative or are they risk-takers?). Understanding your customer personas will inform the people who represent you and help them build long-lasting relationships with end users.

Prepare for Turnover

Create training and development with the assumption there will be new hires constantly coming on board. That means producing programs specifically for the "newbies," introducing them to the basics first. The better your onboarding is, the easier it is for you in the long term.

T3 (Train the Trainer)

If you employ learning and development professionals, they need to be trained, as well. Individuals deployed to educate your sales and service channel must be prepared to represent the brand and differentiation in the strongest and most consistent manner possible. Their messaging, as well as the way they present themselves, must be in lockstep as they are the brand in the eyes of the people being trained.

Our team developed a launch event for a well-known brand. Their lead trainer was charismatic and flamboyant. As "Jake" was delivering one of his virtuoso performances, standing next to me was a young, mesmerized junior trainer who turned to me and said, "I just love to see Jake perform. I have no idea what he's saying, but I like listening to him." Funny comment, but, ideally, you want both a great trainer and a powerful, consistent message to bring your brand and product differentiation to life!

Blend It

Consider which media or execution models are best to deliver your education and development. In-person training can be effective, but what if your facilitator becomes ill or eventually retires? Online classes can be powerful as well, but they require participants to access technology. Printed pieces, videos, work groups, and events are all options to consider. No one type of training fits all, and often a combination of media works best.

Train and Promote You

Educate about your products and technology, but if an employee or dealer doesn't truly value the brand itself, it's a wasted investment for all. Train the enterprise on your exciting vision, resources, company history, worldwide locations (if it has them), environmental commitment, corporate responsibility, and culture. Give people powerful reasons to believe in the brand.

Kia Motors produces new employee training that not only includes product information, but also showcases the company and what it stands for. Included is inspiring education on Kia's technology, worldwide reach, and environmental stewardship, all designed to introduce new hires to the special company they now represent.

Army of Specialists

To turn around their dealers' lackluster sales performance, Greg Smith, then an executive at Audi of America, proposed a "crazy idea" to his superiors. His vision was to train and motivate one salesperson, a *brand specialist*, at each Audi dealership. He felt it was far more effective to shower attention on one individual at retail who believed in the brand rather than on a handful who didn't care.

His laser-beam approach moved those selected to "live" the brand and consequently, Audi sales increased dramatically. Decades later, his program is still in place, with thousands of proud Audi Brand Specialists representing and selling their models.

Ask More

Far too often, companies are reluctant to demand much of their channel when it comes to training. *Ask more and you'll get their attention.* We recommend that prior to any in-person event, you require pre-work. Pre-work may include the participant being certified on your technology, conducting a video walkaround of a new product, or suggesting a solution to a customer experience issue.

That effort, in advance of an event, will provide positive momentum as all will have been involved and contributing. Let's face it, participants should not be at training meetings expecting to be entertained or coddled. *It's a two-way street; the brand invests, and the trainee engages.* This leads to an extraordinarily positive outcome.

Personalize

Since your enterprise likely has people with varying levels of knowledge, experience, and tenure, give them the gift of personalized learning paths. Show you value their time and potential by providing training specific to their role or level of expertise.

Mobile Learning

Make all online or virtual training *mobile friendly*. People are on the go. Meet them where they are by providing accessible education anywhere, any time on their smartphones or tablets.

Two inspiring stories of successful training:

Pulse It

A worldwide manufacturer was preparing to launch a product representing a new segment for the brand and dealer network. They knew they would be in for a dogfight since they were up against very tough, entrenched competitors.

We suggested that rather than producing the standard training program, they follow a different strategy. The typical approach would have entailed emailing online product modules to dealer salespeople prior to launch, hoping they'd be prepared to stand in front of thousands of customers and sell a product they hadn't been familiar with previously. We felt that was a tough ask.

Due to the magnitude of the situation, we recommended they initiate "pulsed" training *eleven* months prior. This vision included not only product education but in addition, a *gamified*, friendly competition amongst the brand's dealerships that would capture their attention and hearts.

Each month, dealers were assigned a task or challenge to complete. For example, one month we'd ask them to research competitive brands and create a "pro and con" presentation. Thirty days later, their assignment was to invite current customers to the dealership to elicit their opinions on the new soon-to-be-released model. This resulted in not only some great insights, but also in hundreds of pre-sales. It also afforded dealers the freedom to invite *all* departments of their retail operations to participate, which improved teamwork.

The launch culminated as each dealership submitted videos of them experiencing competitive products. Imagine the excitement of dealers in eighty-three countries worldwide, from Chile to Austria to Boise, all competing as they learned and mastered this new product segment, together.

Sure, some tasks focused on the upcoming product, but going beyond that and making it hands-on by promoting collaboration within the dealership propelled this launch to be among the brand's most successful in its century of existence.

Cheers

The Macallan is the world's premier Scotch whisky brand, with some bottles fetching over $1 million at auction. While it is a 200-year-old, storied icon, it is also well ahead of its time.

Five years before the COVID-19 pandemic forced the business world to embrace virtual communications, Charlie Whitfield, Global Consumer and Internal Advocacy Lead, announced his vision to create a global online education hub for the brand. He christened it *The Macallan Academy*. Our team jumped at the chance to work with Charlie and this extraordinary brand.

While the idea of a virtual academy was brilliant, with interactive classes and downloadable resources, he went a step further by focusing *first* on training the brand's employees before distributors or others were invited to join. The Macallan team members learned about the brand's rich heritage, distilling process, the exceptional sherry-seasoned oak casks, and the whisky's natural colors, along with scores of other fascinating insights that brought its differentiation and value to light.

Everyone, including leadership, sales, marketing, accounting, and administrative employees, enrolled. They gained confidence, inspired by The Macallan's incomparable craftsmanship and creativity. Then the Academy was launched to distributors, stores, and restaurants worldwide.

Charlie and our team have now trained and certified thousands globally in twelve languages, including French, Japanese, Turkish, and Vietnamese. The Macallan Academy has grown so successfully that each year, dozens of new classes are added to further the learning and grow the passion. Cheers for the brilliant idea, Charlie!

Training and education can be fun and inspiring. Spread the word and ignite passion for your brand throughout the enterprise, and the world!

CHAPTER 18

ACQUIRING A BRAND?

I'VE BEEN FORTUNATE TO WORK with some of the world's most brilliant, successful private equity professionals. These leaders value the physical assets along with the reputation, legacy, and differentiation of the brands they purchase.

Here are our six steps to maximizing an acquisition:

1. **View the sales channel through a different lens than you do the manufacturing operations**. When acquiring a manufacturer, their distribution network is often a point of focus and concern for PE firms. B2B sales channels often seem unsophisticated and slow. Dealers, distributors, or reps may be viewed as "living off" the manufacturer, providing little value. Sometimes true, sometimes not.

   While there may be thoughts of eliminating the sales and service channel after the company is acquired, this seldom works. And just as dangerous is communicating the possibility of it, which is a guarantee of lost revenue, as the best dealers will likely choose to leave and represent your competitors if they get wind of that possibility. Here's a story to illustrate this.

A healthcare brand was acquired, and immediately, new ownership decided to eliminate what they considered frivolous, unneeded marketing investments. One of those was an education program for healthcare providers, who were also the primary purchasers of the brand. Those training courses were extremely popular, engaging and enlightening providers about the product's many functions.

As with many budget reductions, there was no immediate negative effect. But over the following decade, sales dropped precipitously as the next generation of providers no longer bonded with the brand. In the meantime, ownership unsuccessfully sought to gain back the lost market share by reducing price, increasing sales commissions, and other far more costly considerations. The company had alienated their channel and the healthcare provider. The acquisition never achieved its potential.

In most cases, it's wiser to resist any immediate changes and attempt to reignite the channel by listening to and learning from them first. They'll hold invaluable knowledge of the brand and competition. In short order, you'll hopefully partner with them to raise standards and performance. The channel can be a company's greatest asset.

2. **Embrace operational efficiency if it doesn't threaten brand differentiation.** Operational efficiencies are at the heart of the most brilliant acquisition strategies, but just as critical is identifying and protecting differentiation. Efforts to make the acquired company more profitable could dilute or even eliminate product uniqueness, eventually diminishing customer loyalty and competitive edge.

   When streamlining goes too far, it can have disastrous effects on a brand. After GM's acquisition of Saab in 1990, it stripped away the personality of the car. Saab met its ultimate demise in 2011.

A brand that erases its personality not only loses loyal customers, but along with that the confidence of employees, as it no longer is a point of pride for those who design, build, and represent it. Employees and dealers personally identify with their brand if they are proud of it. Take that away and those important individuals no longer are soldiers in your army fighting the battle every day.

3. **Leverage any trade name challenges as a springboard to brand rejuvenation**. *What's in a name?* Often after acquisition, the use of the brand name or logo will be restricted or no longer possible. This is common and can be successfully navigated.

   Our firm was contacted on the very day a well-known truck manufacturer was acquired by a private equity firm. We learned its well-established, century-old logo was now "on the clock." Per the licensing agreement, new ownership had two years to create a new identity. The private equity team wisely used this to their advantage and initiated the process immediately. This afforded time to not only create their new logo but also to build excitement and rally the employees and dealers.

   A new name and logo identity for the acquired brand can become a major element of an overall strategy that includes a relaunch—the perfect opportunity to honor the brand and re-engage employees, customers, and the industry.

4. **Differentiation *after* acquisition is necessary**. Post-acquisition is an ideal time to discover and promote the brand's distinction. A family-owned manufacturer, for example, may have been successful for decades but at a loss as to why. It might be a specialized process, design, or innovative technology. Now that you have acquired the brand, identify and maximize it.

   After an aerospace manufacturer was purchased, new ownership looked to further maximize its investment. As their specialty was explored, it became clear they had a powerful, inspiring differentiation: their proud workforce of military veterans. That skill, expertise, and dedication to our country became the centerpiece of the brand. A new logo and brand messaging were created to reflect that, which grew employee pride while adding to the overall value of the acquisition.

5. **Communicate acquisition messaging to current employees** *first*. Connecting immediately with your newly "acquired" employees is best because they will have endured months of rumors leading up to it. Even after the transaction is finalized, there will still be concern, fear, and skepticism throughout the organization. Open, transparent communication will be far better than none.

   We assisted one of the nation's leading private equity firms and witnessed firsthand the right way to communicate during an acquisition. They were purchasing a struggling manufacturer and considering relocating operations.

   Displaying peerless integrity, their leader was honest with employees, frankly sharing the intent to consolidate and close the plant. He could have been vague or implied the factory might remain open but was truthful and aided the employees in finding new jobs. Consequently, the transition proceeded smoothly and positively. The leader and his firm took the high road and did the right thing for all involved.

6. **Don't cut corners in hiring the best team to run your acquisitions; don't cut corners in branding, either**. It takes a great deal of confidence and expertise to ensure a successful acquisition. However, that confidence can sometimes lead to a do-it-yourself approach to marketing and branding.

   As much consideration should go into discovering your acquisition's differentiation as it does into revamping operations. Quickly cobbling together logos and marketing without an informed strategy leads to inconsistency and diminishes brand value.

We had the pleasure of working with a well-known flooring company that had decided to refresh their numerous brand logos. Despite having strong in-house creative talent, their marketing leader, "Annie," reached out to my team to generate some new ideas. In a matter of several days, we presented dozens of potential identities to her. Within a week, Annie and the team had chosen the "winners" and proceeded to promote and market them going forward using their in-house resources. This effective approach was fun, collaborative, and used both internal and external talent.

Acquisitions can result in extraordinary success stories. Improving operational efficiency while maximizing brand differentiation is a winning combination.

C H A P T E R   1 9

THE TWELVE TRUTHS TO CHANNEL PASSION AND SUCCESS

"I'M GOING TO PLAY HARDBALL with our dealer network. They make too much money off us and need to realize they can all be replaced in a heartbeat." Those words were spoken by the leader who was just installed as CEO of a multi-billion-dollar enterprise. I sat in his boardroom watching the expressions on the faces of his executive team, which ranged from surprise to horror.

At first, his words appeared prophetic as the channel cowered and caved to his bravado. But slowly, the strongest dealers exited the brand to represent the competition. Profit plummeted and market share fell. The CEO was ousted—but not before his actions seriously damaged relationships with the very people who had represented and loved the brand, their dealers.

Great manufacturers produce great products. Great dealers sell products and build great relationships. This is a powerful combination. While there are other models, it is usually risky to unplug your distribution and wiser to draw them in as deeply as possible.

We have compiled our top twelve learnings gleaned from working with hundreds of brands and thousands of dealers across dozens of industries. We actually created a small booklet of "The Twelve Truths" that we share with clients to help them stay on track. These apply to consumer and industrial brands equally, guiding my team daily, and I hope they are as valuable to you.

Here are the Twelve Truths to Channel Performance and Passion:

Truth 1

No matter the strength of your brand, product, or service, if the people who represent it don't genuinely believe in it, you're losing ground.

This is true for all people in any position across an entire enterprise. If dealers do not believe, you're in trouble. If your employees don't either, you're doomed. Sometimes, leaders create a problem that cascades throughout the organization.

An automotive brand was introducing its newest product, their most expensive yet. Expectations had been high, but the launch was now on its deathbed. I was called in to resuscitate it. We interviewed dealer principals who told us the new model was *too premium,* overpriced, and just didn't "fit the brand." Their salespeople openly shared that sentiment with prospective customers, and sales were understandably sluggish.

The brand's regional field force was also opposed to the new product. Up until then, their previous launches were wildly successful, so it was perplexing where this negativity originated. Soon, the source was revealed.

As I spoke with the president of the company, he confided he did not believe in the product and could not imagine it succeeding. I was stunned, asking if he had shared that sentiment with anyone else. He quickly replied, "Well, of course. I told my leadership team and our entire field force that it wasn't a *good fit* for the brand." This was almost verbatim what we were hearing from their dealers, sales team, and field force. The president's doubt had unleashed a chain reaction throughout the enterprise. Was it the wrong product for the brand or a brilliant, bold breakthrough that deserved great success? All we'll ever know is that the product launch was dead on arrival, a failure.

Shortly after its production was cancelled, that automobile became a collector's piece as celebrities quickly snatched it up at high prices. I too, jumped in and purchased two different models and loved them. It wasn't all that bad of a car after all. But the president, and ultimately those in the enterprise, simply did not believe in it. And it, *and they*, failed.

Truth 2

If you compete against an inferior brand, yet their channel is fully engaged, you're in for a battle.

We often hear from a client that a weaker competitor is "eating their lunch." While the competitor's product may not be superior, it is more probable their team and distribution channel are deeply committed and, in the trenches, fighting to win.

And note that even if a dealer offers only your product in its segment, don't fool yourself that they are "dedicated." They can focus their time and effort on other products and services. Your goal is to be their favorite, their priority, and smartest, most lucrative investment of time.

We worked with North American Van Lines and learned that one of their agents, in an effort to increase profit, had started up their own side business. The business? A DJ (disc jockey) service, for weddings! At first it sounded funny, but it revealed that the agent's primary focus wasn't on selling North American's moving services. The energy and effort he spent on that bizarre side hustle diminished and crippled the brand's market share in the region.

Truth 3

The experience at the dealership should be as inspiring as the product and technology being sold and serviced there.

Customers don't distinguish between the brand and the dealer. It's all *one experience* for them. They will judge harshly and abandon a great brand if their dealership encounters are lackluster. And top dealers suffer as well when their underperforming brethren give the brand a black eye.

Imagine a high-tech, premium brand offered at retail nationwide. But the service is uninspired as are their outdated stores and technology. Customers end up disappointed and disillusioned. Both the dealer and brand underperform. No one wins in this scenario. I've seen this occur when companies with amazing potential cut corners to meet profit targets or avoid conflict with their retail partners by allowing substandard performance. Your experience *is* your brand to your customers.

Justin Humphreys, former VP of Sales at Airstream, tackled this. He wanted to elevate the standard of customer experience provided by their dealer network. Partnering with Justin, we created *Five Rivet* Dealer Standards. Inspired by the fact that an iconic Airstream travel trailer is built with an average of 3,000 rivets, only those dealers that meet Airstream's five customer service promises can be recognized as a Five Rivet dealer. Justin's passion to refine the experience at retail encouraged the best dealers to invest further in facilities, technology, and training, enhancing the sales and service experience. In return, those top performers were rewarded with preferred product allocation and special recognition on the brand's website.

Truth 4

Whenever there is a lack of communication or information, people will fill that void with negativity. Avoid the void.

"We don't have all the information yet, so we'll wait before we tell the employees anything." It's typical to hear this from well-intentioned leaders, but, unfortunately, it's a recipe for disaster.

Openly express that you may not know something but will share it when you do. Address the "invisible elephant" issues that everyone expects you to sidestep. If you don't, they will fill the vacuum of information with negative assumptions or even conspiracy theories. Surprise (and inspire) your team by *avoiding the void.*

For years, a truck manufacturer faithfully emailed weekly product communications to dealers to keep them updated on new or improved features. To save money, the program was canceled. Soon damage control was needed as dealers began receiving trucks with new features and assumed they were the wrong units or incorrect orders. This created a firestorm of confusion and frustration that took weeks to untangle. That misguided budget-saving move cost the manufacturer credibility and time, and was an embarrassment.

Truth 5

The moment more than one person, one dealer, or one customer learns of a new product creation, that launch has begun.

Today, with social media dominating our communications, you must assume that as soon as you signal intent to launch a new offering, there will be inquiries, interest, potential sales opportunities, and the *possibility of losing customers.*

A leading brand announced a revolutionary new electric vehicle and assigned it a launch date of approximately one year in the future. Immediately, intrigued consumers began calling and visiting dealers nationwide. Because the exact product specifications were not yet determined, the brand hadn't communicated that vital information. This created a major problem. Dealers were being peppered by customers with questions: "What will be its range?" or "Will it be safe?" That inspired the brand's more "creative" dealers to begin concocting their own answers. Depending on who they asked, customers were told the range for the product was anywhere from 50 to 500 miles fully charged. As for safety, one dealer principal told his customers that the product was safe unless the charging system blew up, warning them, "If that happens, keep in mind you'll be sitting right above the battery."

The channel created their own answers because the manufacturer had not provided information. All this confusion led to many customers losing interest and purchasing rival brands, while others who waited and eventually experienced the product found the dealers' claims to be inaccurate and moved on, disappointed. All of this hurt the product's success and was a setback for the brand.

Once it's known you have a new product planned, begin communicating. And if you don't have every answer, refer to Truth 4 by sharing what you do and don't know now so that you can *avoid the void*.

Truth 6

Your channel can act as an evangelist or as an anarchist. Choose one.

You must align your sales channel to a singular vision; otherwise, they are free agents looking only to close sales and grab the commission, even at the expense of your brand.

I interviewed a top-selling sales agent of North American Van Lines and asked him to share the secret to his success. He enlightened me. "The moving company has a special program that offers a 15 percent discount to charitable associations like United Way or the NAACP. I've decided to make that my focus, and I now sell to more associations than any other salesperson in the nation!" Leaning forward he smiled. "I'm fortunate that most of my customers are members of the HRS, so they get the 15% discount and I get the full sales commission."

I wasn't familiar with that non-profit and asked him what the HRS was, exactly. He replied, "It's *The Human Race Society*. It's funny how just about everyone is a member." To serve his needs, he had discounted the value of the North American brand. And to top it off, his fellow agents were irritated with him for manipulating the system. It's an entertaining story, but it shows what is lost when the sales channel represents itself at the expense of the brand.

In 2016, the Consumer Financial Protection Bureau fined Wells Fargo $100 million for the "widespread illegal practice of secretly opening unauthorized accounts." My wife and I were victims of that fraud and learned of it after receiving a credit card that we had not ordered.

Over 5,000 Wells Fargo employees were fired for that fraudulent activity. This corruption severely damaged their reputation and customer relationships, all in an effort to exceed sales quotas at any cost.

Truth 7

The most effective way to demonstrate your brand's technology is through utilizing technology.

Too many brands tout how advanced their products are, yet their enterprise can't effectively demonstrate it. Progressive manufacturer, Land Rover, equips dealers with digital tablets such as iPads to bring their product to life in ways that a print brochure can't. The pharmaceutical brand, Eli Lilly, allows physicians to don virtual reality (VR) headsets as they visualize Lilly's medicine on its journey throughout a patient's bloodstream.

In 2015, Volvo Cars re-entered the U.S. market with new, highly advanced models. The problem was that their dealership sales and service personnel were not comfortable demonstrating them. The technology was new, as previous Volvo models had been far more basic. At training events nationwide, we held Technology Relay Races, where dealership teams competed by performing tasks such as operating the navigation system or setting up Bluetooth in timed races.

It was fun and lucrative for all. Dealer personnel mastered the Volvo technology, enabling them to be more comfortable demonstrating it and, in thousands of cases, *selling it* to the customers entering their stores daily.

Truth 8

Often, the most formidable barrier that companies and their channels face is overcoming their prior success.

"We sometimes sit around and wonder where all our success comes from. It's amazing how remarkable we are." That was an actual quote from a leader at an iconic brand. Years later, his replacement called me asking for emergency help to re-engage the dealer network.

Previously the envy of their industry, they now woke up to find low employee morale and dealer defection, as customer retention was also plummeting. They asked me to review their dealer training program and to my surprise, I learned that they had been training salespeople *not* to sell products, instead suggesting they wait until the customer tracked them down (hard to believe but true). This was certainly a "sleeping giant" company that became comfortably numb and complacent. It took years to regain momentum.

Success can demotivate us to grow, learn, or listen. Triumphs, like the weather, are temporary. It's best to stay hungry.

Truth 9

A new product and its brand are best launched together... from the inside out.

Every day, brands will launch products as stand-alone initiatives. And, unfortunately, after that launch ends, so does the momentum. Ideally, since any new product should embody what your brand and differentiation are all about, you must view every new product launch as the opportunity to relaunch the brand as well. And best of all, combining them is cost-effective.

Our team of Harrison Swift, Partner, and Natalie Gibble, Account Manager, saw an opportunity for a bus brand as their new zero-emissions product launch neared. They recommended the company seize that opportunity by showcasing their other low-emissions offerings, strongly positioning them as a leader in that segment. This move was a wise one as it promoted the entire product line in addition to reinforcing their historic leadership in alternative energy.

Truth 10

***Change, buy-in, and true progress start at the heart.
Brands and the people who represent them crave meaning
and purpose.***

As you communicate and celebrate with the enterprise, it's crucial that the message has depth: it's not just about making money. Show how the brand makes a difference in the world, or at least in the lives of your customers and employees. No line worker or dealership maintenance person cares about your profitability or shareholder ROI. They rightfully care about themselves, their family, community, co-workers, and customers. Share how your company makes a difference for those individuals.

The channel must be in harmony with the brand to ensure success. When assisting our clients with engaging their networks, we never ask their dealers, "What do you want from the brand to sell this new product?" We instead get to the heart of it, and ask, "Would you like to be an *architect* and partner on this upcoming launch? If so, what needs to be accomplished by dealers like yourself as well as the brand to make it a success for all?"

The brand is not there to order the dealer around, nor to entertain or please them. Both are partners, dedicated to each other to serve their customers, employees, and communities.

Truth 11

***As you amplify the differentiation of your brand, product,
service, or technology, you intensify the engagement of your
channel and customers.***

No one ever tattooed the name of a commodity on their body. But plenty of body parts with tattoos proudly display Harley-Davidson, the Marines, and other inspiring brands. The more you identify and celebrate what makes you distinct, the more likely you'll stand out, inspire, and grow relationships with those who believe in you. You want your brand *tattooed* on the hearts of all who touch it.

As we were conducting research for a manufacturer, we ran into conflicting information. Dealers uniformly complained about the poor condition of the product shipped to them. Conversely, their customers *raved* about the brand's amazing quality.

There was no disconnect in our research. Instead, it illustrated the role a brand-loyal dealer can play in protecting your image. The manufacturer, under pressure to meet sales targets, was shipping flawed products overflowing with quality issues to dealerships. The proud dealers, however, jumped in and fixed every issue, ensuring the unit was perfect *prior* to customer delivery. Only the dealer knew what they had to go through to achieve that feat.

The manufacturer soon woke up to this and improved their internal quality standards, in part because the dealers were charging them to fix those mistakes—after all, they are dealers in business as well!

Truth 12

If you're comfortable, you're not growing. This applies to brands and people.

Discovering your differentiation may require discomfort. If you're not a little uncomfortable, then you and your brand are not growing. Inviting customers, suppliers, and employees to share their opinions on your product can sometimes sting, but, often, invaluable insights result. Even better, when you genuinely show respect to them while doing this, it dramatically increases their sense of loyalty.

While interviewing dealers of a leading truck manufacturer, we came across intriguing anecdotes. The first dealer proudly shared. "I asked for a specific ladder attachment thirty years ago, and they actually built it for me. I feel it was really my design." Another chimed in, saying, "That ladder accessory that has become so popular? Well, that was my idea. I played a part in its success." And yet, another dealer had their own story: "They talked with me twenty years ago and asked for suggestions to boost sales. I told them to modify the ladder, and they actually listened. I love that they valued my input."

Who exactly deserves credit for the ladder idea? It doesn't matter. What's certain is this brand cultivated fiercely loyal dealers who genuinely believe they are integral to its success. How could they ever imagine representing or selling another brand? This illustrates the dividends reaped when asking for, listening to, and acting on input from your dealers.

The brand with an engaged channel is formidable, and that's the truth!

CHAPTER 20

UP FOR THE CHALLENGE?

ONE OF THE MOST COURAGEOUS and effective ways to demonstrate your differentiation is by pitting it against the competition. My company has conducted competitive challenge events for products ranging from cars to TV sets to mobility vans to fire hose nozzles (yes, fire hose nozzles). And if done properly, assuming your product is strong, you can be a winner, *even if you don't finish in first place.*

The following are stories and suggestions to help ensure your competitive comparison events are most successful.

"The People's Challenge"

In the late 1990s, Volkswagen approached us. They had a product that was not selling. They truly thought their model was strong, yet it received little interest from dealers or customers. This was my company's first chance to work with the great brand, so we jumped in. By visiting dealerships in search of answers, we immediately found that many were not offering test drives of the model because they didn't believe in it. Not to overstate the obvious, but if a salesperson will not let a customer test drive a car, it's highly unlikely they'll buy it. I knew we were onto something. We just had to find to a way inspire salespeople to believe in the VW product.

My team huddled and brainstormed on hundreds of possible solutions to help this car sell. We landed on what would become a proprietary product for us. Our inspiration was to create the ideal shopping *and learning* experience for the customer. Instead of them having to drive across town to various dealers to test drive cars, we would hold an event at one location for them to experiment with the competitive cars right there. This would give the VW model a fair chance to be pitted against the competitive set, and we were convinced it would perform quite well. Our plan was to videotape the entire experience and package it as training for dealers, hopefully influencing them to actually offer test drives and ideally, sell the car. But we knew we first had to persuade our client to give us permission for this ambitious concept.

We hurriedly produced a video with our employees acting out the parts of customers or dealers, as a demonstration (or rough idea) that I could present to the client. In retrospect, the presentation was primitive and amateurish, but it had passion.

I met with the client, played the video, and shared our idea: *Let's give the VW model a chance to compete fairly. No doubt it'll do well against Honda or Toyota, right? We'll then package it as a training program to educate and motivate salespeople across the nation. They'll believe in it because they saw consumers fall in love or at least fall in "like" with it.*

I turned to the client for his response. He was speechless as his face turned red. I knew I either hit the bullseye or he was about to throw me out of the building. Luckily, it was the former. Courageously, he supported our idea and said, "Do it!" This was a "big break" for my company and with no exaggeration, changed our future, for the better.

The People's Challenge, our proprietary competitive comparison product, was born! Our team traveled to an abandoned water park in California to set up shop and orchestrate the ultimate car-buying experience. We invited scores of consumers to drive and learn about the top models in the mid-size car segment, including Honda, Toyota, BMW, Mazda, and our client's VW. Participants were given the opportunity to push the cars to the limit (safely) utilizing skid pads and a gymkhana (think of it as an obstacle course for cars).

In addition, all were educated on each model's warranties, specifications, mileage, and reliability. We even staged a fun competition to determine which car had the most useable trunk space. Participants were provided luggage, bags, and boxes and then challenged to "pack" the trunks to discover which one held the most. That's something you'd never get to do at the dealership!

The four-hour event had one "secret"—no one was told that VW had sponsored it. We simply said my firm was conducting the experience to gauge consumer perceptions. So, people arrived excited to drive cars and share their opinion freely without pressure to buy. Another fascinating touch was asking each person to share their perceptions throughout the day to see if trends were emerging as they became more informed. We tracked that data and revealed much of it at the event's conclusion.

For example, our Volkswagen client was initially concerned when participants ranked his product at rock bottom in every category at the beginning of the event. We told him this was good news, and it was, for the VW rose in stature as people experienced it throughout the day. At the conclusion of the event, we shared the results with the participants. VW, as we expected, was not the most popular product but was voted "the brand that surprised me the most" and "the car I'd most likely purchase." All this was captured on videotape for dealership training, which dramatically improved perceptions at retail, as sales then took a turn for the better.

This project spurred us to conduct similar competitive comparisons for dozens of clients. I'll share much of what we've learned. Consider these strategies if you are brave enough to enter the battle.

Blind Taste Test

Most competitive comparison events are not "blind," but if you can conceal the identity of the brands, go for it. This allows customers to experience products without the bias of knowing their identities or seeing their logos. It's easier to do this if you produce a baked good (such as bread) or a component. It is difficult, but possible, if you're dealing with highly recognized brands in the automotive or trucking industries, for example.

Embrace (Actually, Love) Being the Underdog

My company's most successful comparison events occurred when our client's product was the "underdog." When a brand is the underachiever, yet is a strong offering, it has the power to surprise people with how well it performs against the segment leaders, sometimes becoming a favorite in the eyes of the customer.

As shared earlier, we conducted a competition for a Volkswagen model. Our client was nervous about the outcome, as the car would be positioned against formidable, higher-selling brands such as Honda, Toyota, and even BMW. But the VW had an advantage: it was the underdog. Expectations for it were low, yet it performed impressively in the eyes of the customers. People root for the underdog.

Create the Ideal Purchase Experience

The most powerful comparisons allow participants to touch, feel, and study the products, far beyond what they would be able to do in the usual buying environment. When helping an upstart electronics brand evaluate its big screen TV against Sony, Samsung, and others, we invited consumers to push the products to the extreme, toying and playing with every feature offered. After hours of intense experimentation, these consumers gained invaluable insights into each product, far more than they'd have gained at a big-box store walking the aisles. The brand's features held their own against the well-known brands, surprising the participants and leading to increased market share.

Warts and All

No product is perfect, including yours. The only true competitive event is an honest one. Present each product (yours and the competition's) objectively, including all strengths or weaknesses. You'll soon see how important those shortcomings are (or aren't) in the eyes of the customer. When we produced comparison events for Holiday Rambler RVs, we not only showcased the strengths of their product but also openly shared the impressive attributes of their competitors, which added to the credibility of the experience.

Track Perceptions

Realize that a competition is not a winner-take-all situation. It's all about how customer perceptions shift throughout the experience. Your goal is to see your product "move up" in their eyes from the beginning to the conclusion of the event. If it exceeded expectations, you have won and that needs to be celebrated and leveraged.

Finish Second (or Third) and Win

Sure, the top-selling product in your segment is likely to be a winner at the end of the comparison event. It ought to be. But if your product rose from fifth to second place in the category of "best product for the price" and participants voted it as the product "I'd most likely purchase," congratulations, you've done well and (I love this) your competition will be very upset!

Memorialize It

Interview participants on video during and after your competitive event. Their verbatims often are priceless, providing a fascinating perspective. There's nothing more powerful than a customer sharing how much your product impressed them. Use their words to help your brand grow.

We videotaped an event featuring customers sharing how our client's product exceeded their expectations. Then we packaged it as a training piece for the sales channel. Years later, dealer salespeople were still reciting those powerful customer quotes in their sales presentations.

What If We Lose and Get Crushed?

That's a question we often hear. It's a fair one. If after conducting a comparison event you were the *grand loser*, you have many options. Perhaps you learn from it and take that input to improve the product and brand. You can always scrap it and press "delete" as if it never happened. The truth is, in our decades of conducting these events, not one of our clients shut down the program; they all used it to position their brands positively.

Be Independent

If you plan to publish and promote the event's results in marketing, you must ensure a level playing field, or your competitors will cry foul. In those cases, we employ an independent third-party accounting firm to audit the results. And it's smart for clients to avoid influencing the outcome. Once, an overzealous CEO pried his way into conversations (on video) with customers during an event (they had no idea who he was). His team wisely dragged him away.

Waivers

If you capture the event on video and plan to use it for training or other purposes, make sure the participants sign legal waivers. One time, at a Volkswagen event, a participant became nervous when he saw the cameras and panicked. He turned to our client and begged to leave, telling us, "I can't be caught on camera, I'm wanted by the law." I don't know if that was true, but we gladly paid him his fee and allowed him to depart.

If you have the courage to compare your product against its competitive set, kudos to you. Be willing to accept any shortcomings as you step back, watching others judge your product. And if you are the underdog, all the better because you can't really lose.

The key is to share the stories of your product's performance, how it exceeded expectations and stood up to a far more expensive competitor with all who represent or touch your brand, including employees, your sales channel, and customers.

CHAPTER 21

COMMUNICATE AND CELEBRATE

AFTER IDENTIFYING YOUR DIFFERENTIATION and launching new branding, you must continue to *strike up the band* by celebrating what makes you who you are. People need to be constantly reminded of and inspired by what your brand represents. Your employees' lives are filled with noise that warns them of impending danger that they have no power over—worldwide upheaval, politics, pandemics, and conspiracy theories. *One of the few areas of control and power they have is in choosing where they work and how much they care about the job they do.*

If your investment in differentiation saw you make only small gains in market share but rallied the organization around your brand, that alone would represent an extraordinary success as you'd benefit from their improved performance, retention, and engagement. As all that occurred, your customer loyalty would certainly skyrocket. It would be a challenge to *not* grow your business!

It's that simple and that hard: differentiating your brand makes complete sense but it won't just fall into your lap. It requires constant attention and discipline. Here are examples illustrating this point from our Brand Re-Engineering interviews—two employees from different companies, each with dramatically diverse viewpoints of their brands.

One told me, "I heard we just landed a new customer. I guess they must have liked us or maybe we had the lowest price, who knows? Unfortunately, now we have more pressure to get stuff done; it's going to be a crappy next few months."

The other said, "I was approached by a marshmallow factory across town, offering me twenty-five cents more an hour. I'm not going to take it; I'd rather help save lives than make marshmallows."

These two quotes illustrate the chasm between an employee who is "mailing it in" and one who is loving and living the brand.

The first, surprisingly, was from the Chief Operating Officer at a technology company. He was passive, burdened by a new opportunity his company landed. That type of disengagement is inevitable unless we continually remind people of what makes us unique.

The second quote is from a line worker after turning down a higher-paying job. A proud quality control manager at an ambulance manufacturing plant, she truly believes she's saving lives.

One person is dealing with the inconvenience of a new customer while the other is in the *lifesaving business*. These examples show that people without purpose are rudderless while others who know they make a difference are proud and involved. Leaders must constantly remind our most valuable asset—our people—that they are doing something significant and are appreciated.

- Do your employees assemble wire harnesses, or do they make ambulances that help save the lives of thousands of people?
- Do they tighten bolts, or do they build the coolest motorcycles in the world?
- Do they construct components, or do they engineer safety innovations that protect truck drivers?
- Do they make HVAC systems, or are they preserving our environment?
- Do they work at a local marketing firm, or do they discover what makes a brand special and help them celebrate it?

Our Ugly, Top-Selling Car

The president of a major auto manufacturer was stressing out over a make-or-break new car launch. The stakes were high, and it was already going poorly.

He called me up pleading, "I need help—we have a lousy, ugly car that no one is buying. We're replacing it with a new model. Morale is low internally; this launch must succeed. Come to my office as soon as possible, this is an emergency." As I began the assignment, my team conducted research on that product that shocked me. Armed with this bombshell, I called the president with a question he was not prepared for and asked, "Can you guess which car was the number one seller in your segment over the last decade?" The president replied, "I don't have the foggiest idea." I then informed him that his brand's current "lousy, ugly car that no one was buying" had been the top-selling model, adding that it was still experiencing strong sales.

Stunned, he replied, "This certainly explains why morale is in the tank. We've denigrated this car, yet it's been a success." He was right. Their employees and dealers had feasted on a diet of negativity about the product instead of showing it the respect it deserved. And, this was not just about a car, it was about the people at the company as well. This constant belittling affected them as it eroded their pride. Together, we began an inspiring journey to turn that around, and it all began with an internal celebration.

There, the president addressed hundreds of employees, confessing that while this car had achieved greatness, it was underappreciated and from that day on, they were going to honor it as they focused on the future. His sincerity was deeply appreciated as the brand moved on to enjoy a highly successful launch.

Next, I'll share how a company enduring severe quality issues captured the hearts of its employees, dealers, and customers.

The Home of Integrity

Established in 1934, Schult Modular Homes was considered a break-through innovator in housing. Founder Wilbur Schult had attended the Chicago World's Fair in 1933 and was inspired when he attended a house trailer exhibit at the fair (today, that doesn't sound interesting at all, but back then affordable, prefabricated housing was considered revolutionary). He returned home to Indiana dedicating himself to building modular homes, which he enthusiastically promoted as a "treasure to freedom and efficiency." For decades, they were a leading housing brand in America. Slowly, over time, however, quality issues eroded their image.

They brought in a leader in 2002, Ervin "Erv" Bontrager, to turn it around. A tough but very open-minded man, his hard-nosed edict to me was, "Look, I don't want to hear any positive stuff. Just find the problems so I can fix them." He was determined to restore Schult to being the "treasure" it once was.

We set out to learn what was not only behind their recent struggles but also to discover their strengths. They had been successful for decades and boasted the best dealers in the nation. They surely had to be doing a lot of things well.

Our team conducted over one hundred interviews with employees, dealers, and customers to discover what the brand truly was. Erv's employees spoke of how their quality had lagged but surprisingly, were proud of the strides being made. Dealers declared likewise, claiming undying loyalty to the brand. This feedback was unexpected because, usually, when a company is experiencing serious quality issues, it results in strained relationships with those who represent it. Then we met with their customers, and it all came together.

I interviewed an elderly woman who shared her Schult story. "My husband and I bought the home, and it did have a few minor issues, which we fixed ourselves. Then one day, there was a disaster. Our plumbing went out, our house flooded, and we were worried sick. I called Schult and told them our plumbing had exploded and we need-ed help now. The very next morning, there was a knock on the door with two fellows from Schult to fix it. They worked for hours and took care of everything. We couldn't thank them enough."

I waited for her to catch her breath and asked, "Why in the world would you be so thrilled that Schult corrected their own problem?" I was stunned by her answer: "Well, the reason I love Schult is that they didn't actually install the plumbing, so it wasn't their issue, but they sent people out to fix it for us anyway."

Unbelievable! This admittedly flawed company dove in to help a customer, even when they had no role in creating the problem they were solving. Time and time again, we heard stories of how Schult helped their customers, even if the issue was not their fault. We had discovered that this was a company that cared, a company with integrity. And not only did customers feel this, so did dealers and employees who were dispatched and paid by Schult to address any customer issue. This was at the heart of what the company was all about, and it had to be shared.

I couldn't wait to tell Erv what we learned. After he heard the stories of how his team was caring for customers no matter the reason, he looked up from his paperwork, leaned forward, and replied, "Well, isn't that the way it should be?" That underscored what kind of leader he was, dedicated to doing the right thing. But where Erv needed a lit-tle help was in telling that story, celebrating it, and inspiring everyone involved with the brand to continue behaving this way.

Schult's differentiation was their commitment to do what's right for the customer. Yes, they were currently rising out of a prolonged slump, and they were nowhere near perfect, but their DNA was overflowing with the right stuff and customers, dealers, and employees knew it. This was especially powerful because in the prefabricated housing in-dustry, plenty of competitors were taking advantage of lower income customers buying modular homes. Instead, Schult showed they valued each one of them.

That tough guy leader showed plenty of emotion as he celebrated their inspiring differentiation with employees and dealers at the annual meeting. There he thanked them for embodying what the brand stood for. For the next two years, we helped Schult train and invigorate the dealer network to communicate and market their differentiation with customers, as it steadily climbed back to prominence.

We created a rally cry that symbolized all we had learned about Schult. That slogan, *The Home of Integrity*, was proudly displayed at their plants and offices to reinforce what they represent. It gives me great pride to see our motto lives on, decades after Wilbur Schult's treasure had been acquired by Berkshire Hathaway, Inc.

Reinforce Your Brand by Celebrating It Inside Your Four Walls

The condition and presentation of your company's facilities send a message to your team. Do any of the following apply?

- You're a premium brand with advanced technology and design, yet your operations look ancient, cluttered, and dirty.

- You're a trusted food manufacturer with a legacy of quality, although your team ignores safety protocols.

- You're a leading division of a conglomerate but no images of your products are displayed throughout the buildings. Instead, walls are "adorned" with outdated photos of the parent company's various brands, none of which are manufactured by your team.

To sustain and ideally build brand momentum, view your facilities as an extension of your brand messaging. Here are recommendations:

Be True

Whether it's in a brochure, on your website, on social media, or on the walls of your offices, never change or modify your branding. It's a fun but damaging exercise to "play around" by altering your logo, slogan, fonts, or brand colors. Faithfully honor brand guidelines by showcasing inspiring photography and messaging throughout all facilities. Memorialize product launches and other important milestones by erecting signage, posters, or banners to let your team know their importance.

Consider Your Audience

Display meaningful messaging in the facilities that goes beyond the standard, but important, safety messages.

My team helped German manufacturer Volkswagen invigorate its Chattanooga, Tennessee, workplace messaging. Initially, our brilliant Germanic clients preferred the theme "Perfection" to be prominently displayed throughout their facility.

We discussed with them that Americans view the term "perfection" far differently than Germans, who aspire to it. Most of us in the U.S. don't find perfection realistic or attainable. We respectfully suggested they alter the theme to "Passion for Detail," which was far more relatable to their line workers and management, who readily embraced it.

Elevator Speeches on Elevators?

One of the most inspiring people I've ever met is the late Steve Neder. He took charge of the new Jetta launch a few decades back, rallying the entire Volkswagen organization around the new model. Steve was always game for unique ideas, so when we suggested that VW employees share their new Jetta "elevator speeches" on the company's elevator doors, he loved it. We created beautiful posters that were affixed to all the elevator doors; it was fun and original. We did have one issue, though. A few of the elevator shafts jammed up as the posters got stuck in them. No problem, we then secured them to nearby walls. Every brand needs a Steve Neder who allows for imperfection in the pursuit of inspiration.

Refuse to Look Like a Commodity

When copper rod producer SDI LaFarga changed their name to COPPERWORKS, their leader Kurt Breischaft was the cheerleader rallying the team to redecorate the facility with fresh, inspiring images of the brand. A copper rod facility can be a daunting place, with furnaces roaring and flames shooting up throughout its dark environment. Kurt focused on where he could make the biggest impression. The exterior of their massive facility was repainted to boldly display their new name and its slogan, *This Is Where Copper Works,* transforming it from looking like a typical, unappealing factory into an inspiring billboard for the brand.

Before

After

Differentiation Stations

Proudly display your uniqueness inside your facility or plant. Throughout a leading bus manufacturer's plant, they constructed "stations" with signage clearly identifying their differentiators. This smart move inspires employees and serves to educate and impress visitors, including customers and suppliers, when touring the plant.

Create the "Tour"

Visiting your operation is a big deal for customers, suppliers, and dealers. Make it interesting and memorable by designing the ideal "tour" for them. Clean it up, erect fresh signage, and encourage your team to play a role in bringing your brand and differentiation to life.

As leaders, our employees rightfully view us as either 1) people who believe and preach the gospel to our teams or 2) "suits" who play the game and don't truly care.

When a facility is in disrepair and we don't address it, that message results in lower quality and morale. Our employees' eyes and ears are tuned in to how we behave. We need to realize they choose to believe or not believe and to care or not to care. Show them you care.

CHAPTER 22

STAY HUNGRY, STAY HUMAN

I'VE BEEN FORTUNATE TO KNOW LEADERS from companies of all sizes, industries, and degrees of success—leaders who are hungry to do better, to grow, to feel a sense of accomplishment and momentum.

I've collaborated with executives who were intimidating in the eyes of their teams, and yet I experienced none of that. I saw them as human beings on a mission with maybe a few rough edges but, deep down, in almost every single case, great people.

Kudos to You

One point I'd like to emphasize is that most of today's leaders truly value their employees. Decades ago, most corporate executives I encountered routinely dismissed the idea of celebrating their brand and differentiation with line workers. Even fewer would consider inviting employees to share their input. Today, enlightened leaders clearly understand that to attract and retain the best workforce, every individual in the enterprise must believe in what they are doing and the brand they represent.

Inspire and Trust

It's easy to put others "in their place" when you're a top executive. But the best leaders do the opposite—they embrace all who affect the brand, including suppliers. Anoop Prakash, EVP Americas, AriensCo, embodies this, propelling brands to achieve beyond their expectations due to his willingness to be vulnerable. He asked my team to conduct Brand Re-Engineering and when we uncovered a sensitive issue, it was immediately quashed by his associate. Upon learning of it, Anoop boldly demanded the topic be openly aired. He was wise, as this one act positively transformed the organization.

"Intensity" and "Passion"

Intensity is the emotion your team feels from you (and may complain about) as you push forward, making sure they are doing the right thing: "I can't believe how intense he is!"

Passion is the inspiring trait of yours that your people describe *after* your company wins the award, meets the sales goal, or lands the big project: "We love his passion, it's amazing!" *Intensity and passion are two sides of the same coin: it's the currency of being a leader.*

Expect "in-the-moment" pushback as you motivate your team to focus on differentiation. Have confidence that once you succeed, they will pat each other on the back as the brand is now in more demand. And maybe one or two people will acknowledge your passion and belief.

Your People are the Answer

Mark Millett and Theresa Wagler have been leaders at Steel Dynamics (SDI) for years. While a steel producer is often viewed as a commodity provider, Mark and Theresa have made it clear their primary focus is on people, not iron ore and scrap. They've brought heart to the steel business with their investment in companywide safety programs and their industry-leading compensation plan, which rewards and cele-brates workforce performance. This passion for people has rewarded SDI stockholders as well as their employees and families.

And on the topic of appreciating employees, I recall when Theresa attended COPPERWORKS' groundbreaking ceremony. The brand (an affiliate of SDI) was bravely investing millions in their facility, despite being in the throes of the pandemic. Theresa addressed the audience, and rather than discuss profit or investment return, she turned to the employees and personally thanked them for their dedication and care, sharing her pride in them. Your people *are* the answer.

Someone's Precious Child

Bob Chapman is a world-renowned author and Chairman of Barry-Wehmiller Companies, a global manufacturing technology and services supplier. His book, *Everybody Matters: The Extraordinary Power of Caring for Your People Like Family,* inspired me to reach out and learn from him.[5] As Bob graciously discussed this book, he stopped in midsentence and said, "Do you realize that every person under a leader's care is someone's precious child, and the way we view them will have a significant impact on how they treat their spouses and children? It is our responsibility to heal the 'poverty of dignity' that is so prevalent today." Bob Chapman's wisdom serves as a powerful reminder of the extraordinary influence leaders can have on the lives of those they lead. By recognizing and honoring the inherent worth of every individual, regardless of their difficulties or shortcomings, we can pave the way for a future where all "precious children" thrive and flourish under our care.

Generous Genius

Dr. Michael Mirro, an acclaimed cardiologist and researcher, embodies both generosity and brilliance. His exceptional contributions have earned him the honor of having a research center named after him. What sets him apart is his unwavering dedication to the well-being of those under his care, extending even to his friends and their acquaintances. Mike readily assumes the role of a "concierge doctor," assisting

---

5   Bob Chapman, *Everybody Matters: The Extraordinary Power of Caring for Your People Like Family* (Alberta, Canada: Portfolio, 20150)

anyone in need of medical care. For him, the primary focus is always on helping others. I am privileged to refer to him as a "Genius" due to his extraordinary intellect, and I am even more proud to call him a cherished friend.

Stand for Your Brand

Johan De Nysschen took the helm of Audi of America and immediately shook things up. Unimpressed with their solid but not segment-leading position, he refused to allow the sales team to discount product to "hit their numbers." Instead, he demanded the entire organization stand up for the brand by commanding the price it deserved. After numerous head shakes and eye rolls from his leaders, Johan persevered. Due to his courage, the brand proceeded to achieve record sales each month for years to come.

Conveniently Wild

Mark Littell was a very successful major league pitcher for nine years in the 1970s and '80s and was a hard-throwing, "conveniently wild" righthander. Mark also authored three hilarious books on his baseball exploits and was an entrepreneur as well, creating *Panther Piss* Hot Sauce and *Nutty Buddy* athletic cups. He led teams and organizations until he passed in 2022. By being true to himself, he never tried to imitate, never claimed to be perfect, but was always genuine. Great leaders exude authenticity and inspire others to join in the game with them.

Rinse and Repeat

As a leader, you must constantly tell the story of your brand and culture. Don't assume that once it's shared, everyone "gets it." Repeat the message with the assumption that this is the first time that person has ever heard it (or the first time they finally paid attention).

Every Day is a Potential Internal Branding Opportunity

Don't wait for the big all-employee meeting to let people know how significant they are. Each seemingly small interaction with your team is an opportunity to help them connect what they are doing with why it's meaningful.

Remember, the idea of your company profiting will inspire only a few in the enterprise. It will be a turnoff for most. Avoid numbers and charts illustrating "throughput" and other metrics that are *yawners*. Get to the heart—your team's hearts.

A CEO was very fired up and told me, "I'm excited to share great news with employees at the plant. Shareholders' return on investment is up, profits are strong, and our stock is skyrocketing. This ought to motivate them!" I countered, "Do you think they really view this as a positive? Why should they be happy you and the executives are making money off them? How about a more powerful message about your investment in new machinery and how it will ensure a safer environment for all?"

Hallmark Cards

In difficult times, be transparent with your team. You'll be respected for telling the unvarnished truth. No one believes or values feel-good "Hallmark Card" announcements that sugarcoat reality, as it will usually be assumed things are far worse than they really are. People value candor and sincerity.

It's Not About Me (or You or Us)

One of the beauties of finding your differentiation is that it provides your enterprise with a purpose, a significance. It's not primarily about the stockholders or leadership making money, it's about producing a product or service in a special way that ultimately makes a difference, a positive one. When you identify that and share the message with your people, you can be bold and unapologetic. At my firm, we clearly understand we are the people who are behind great people (our clients), and our job is to help them meet and surpass their expectations and even, sometimes, their dreams. That message allows us to set high standards because after all, it's not about us, it's about helping our clients and their brands.

Home Cooking

It is possible to create your branding "in-house" and many companies do. But it's difficult to view your uniqueness when you're so close to it. Another challenge with "Home Cooking" (doing all your brand strategy and marketing in-house) is the lack of objectivity because the internal team that creates the work gets to judge it, as well. And guess what? They usually *love* it!

I suggest that a third-party firm tackle your brand discovery, strategy, and the identification of your differentiators. This provides fresh, inspiring creativity that would have been almost impossible to achieve otherwise. After your brand and differentiation are discovered and articulated, the in-house team can then take the ball and run with it. Approaching it this way is initially more expensive than Home Cooking, but is a smart, long-term investment. What will be accomplished, including logo, slogan, positioning, and differentiators, will benefit the company for decades.

In my experience, after our firm begins a branding or differentiation assignment with clients, they'll most often choose to continue with us because we've developed a deep appreciation of the brand and its potential. Moving forward, the in-house team will usually work in tandem with us, applying our templates and guidelines to their day-to-day projects. As an additional advantage, the in-house team will "up" its game while it collaborates with our designers and technologists.

Bandwidth Partnership

Sometimes my firm partners with a client's in-house team, other times we *become* that team and an *extension* of their company. Here are examples:

- ⚡ A distributor asked to outsource all marketing to us, not to reduce headcount, but to allow their people to stop focusing on marketing in their spare time as they tackled sales or customer issues.

- ⚡ A powersports company hired us to play the role of strategists for their training department, providing their programmers with inspired creative content for their learning and development modules.

- ⚡ An iconic brand turned to us to join their launch team to add the resources and creativity needed for a worldwide product introduction.

A few decades ago, when my company was young, North American Van Lines asked me to acquire their in-house marketing team and become their advertising division. It's embarrassing as an entrepreneur to say this, but I just wasn't comfortable taking over a department of a huge corporation, so I declined. This began a sequence of them unsuccessfully asking me to reconsider, as I even went to the effort to introduce and recommend other firms for them to interview.

Finally, after a year of these overtures from them (I remember the exact room I was in and the time of day, vividly), I received a call from the North American VP pleading, "Barry, will you please acquire our marketing department?" Exasperated, I replied, "I've given you the names of a dozen other companies to work with, why do you keep asking me to do this?" He simply replied, "Because we trust you." His response leveled me. I said, "Let's do it" and got off the phone wondering what I had just agreed to. I share this because it shows how clueless I had been to the opportunity as it turned out to be a positive, career-altering decision.

Now, before you assume things went smoothly, I can honestly say what I acquired was close to a disaster. But it educated me on the challenge of in-house departments and how they are often unfair for all concerned. I tackled the assignment immediately, and found I inherited not only their staff, but a backlog of two hundred projects that were in disarray. That problem stemmed from the enterprise looking at the in-house team as order-takers who could not say "no" to any request. This resulted in missed deadlines, subpar work, and a long list of unfinished projects (many of which were no longer viable).

Another challenge was that the people in the department were former truck drivers who dabbled in photography, video, and design. They were "hobbyists" who in the long run were not best suited to execute marketing and media at a professional standard. And surprisingly, many of them told me they were tired of producing work for the moving company. It took a while to get things in order, but for over a decade, my firm successfully partnered with North American. I'm grateful that I finally said, "Let's do it."

Take Time Off to be Human

Today, there is great pressure for leaders to perform and meet expectations. Give yourself time to feel and react as a person, and it will help energize you to fight the antipathy and fear of change you may feel from your team. You'll need that because differentiation doesn't "belong" to one department; it's an enterprise-wide pursuit.

Discovering and celebrating your brand's differentiation may well be one of the most rewarding experiences of your career. Many clients have told me precisely that. Like any great journey, it takes time. You will surely experience a few twists and turns along the way, but, trust me, it will be worth it!

Go forward knowing that you are doing what few do: you're making decisions, focusing on strengths, and rallying the people who represent and choose your brand.

Leaders differentiate.

ACKNOWLEDGEMENTS

AT THE TOP OF THE LIST is my wife, Carol, who has endured and supported me through our business and personal lives. There would be no "LABOV" without her. She's read, cowritten, and edited this manuscript numerous times, correcting my grammar and inspiring me to share more.

My children, Laura and Alan, have been with me through much of this journey, and have given me love and dearly needed perspective along the way.

Our two grandboys, Grayson and Cooper, energize me and, along with Carol, Laura, Alan, and my amazing brother, Dean, are why I am so grateful.

Our employees (many of whom have been introduced in this book) have been invaluable. What a fun group of dedicated, loving, and certainly, creative people! The book is because of them, based on them, and *for* them, celebrating the difference they make for me, our clients, and our community.

I extend my heartfelt gratitude to my "book team" of Carol LaBov, Tamzen Meyer, Alan LaBov, Matt Hakey, Marcus McMillen, Harrison Swift, and Cathy Schannen for their tireless contributions as my partners in the reviewing, editing, and image gathering. They've given me unwavering support throughout this entire process. Their involvement has undeniably elevated the book to new heights. I would also like to acknowledge the exceptional input and guidance provided by Georgette, Deb, River, David, and Emma from the team at Indigo River Publishing. Their insights have shaped and enriched the final outcome, and I am sincerely grateful for their involvement.

I thank my late parents who grounded me (literally, hundreds of times) and built my confidence to believe I could achieve anything I put my mind to.

My faith, which was rekindled by Sister Mary Doolittle decades ago, has been by my side all the way.

And the greatest thank you is to the people who inspired this book, our clients. I have learned far more from them than vice versa. Some of the most fun, most clever, funniest, warmest, most brilliant, and most unusual humans to set foot on earth—those are our clients!

And finally, I acknowledge that much of what I've shared is my opinion or viewpoint, as I'm not a scientist, researcher, or academic. Closer to my background in music, my approach is to follow inspiration; that's exactly how I've constructed this book and why many of the stories were chosen, simply based on what I found to be intriguing, fascinating, and potentially of value to others. I have taken the liberty to omit or change a name or industry, sometimes even combining several stories in order to create one stronger lesson.

That's all I have to say here; nobody but the acknowledged and the person who acknowledges them cares about acknowledgements anyway!

ABOUT THE AUTHOR

BARRY LABOV is the founder and CEO of LABOV Marketing Communications and Training. He is a two-time Ernst & Young Entrepreneur of the Year recipient and an inductee into the Entrepreneur of the Year Hall of Fame. He is also a Better Business Bureau Torch Awards for Ethics recipient. Under his leadership, LABOV Marketing, Communications and Training received the Indiana Growth 100 Award six times, was named small business of the year, and recognized as one of the best places to work. Additionally, LABOV's client work has been honored with nearly 100 national and regional awards.

With the publication of *The Power of Differentiation*, Barry has authored or co-authored over a dozen business books and written over 100 business articles covering a range of topics. He and his wife, Carol, head their own charitable foundation that contributes to worthy causes every year.

Printed in the USA
CPSIA information can be obtained
at www.ICGtesting.com
LVHW011456240624
783874LV00028B/269